Sara's Story

One Family's
Faith through
Unthinkable Trial

TIMOTHY L. CULVER

Sara's Story

*A true story of inspirational recovery,
overcoming the impossible,
and the one book your insurance
company doesn't want you to read*

ISBN 978-1-934749-60-9
Library of Congress Control Number: 2009935572

Dedication

This book is dedicated to the families of stroke victims and stroke survivors. I want them to know hope exists in this life and the next.

I also dedicate this book to First Baptist Church, Sunnyvale, TX. If the Apostle Paul were to write about a church today, he would have most certainly have written about FBC Sunnyvale as a model for others to emulate.

Finally, I dedicate this book to my family. My parents and in-laws have set the example for my children to follow as they go through life. They have set the example the Bible mentions when it says . . . *lest you forget the things your eyes have seen, and lest they depart from your heart all the days of your life. And teach them to your children and grandchildren* . . . (Deut. 4:9).

I also dedicate this book to a great woman—Billie J. Culver, 1932 – 2009. She inspired me to be more than I can be.

Table of Contents

Preface

I've never before tried to actually sit down and write a book. I will confess that I've thought about it many times, but the gap between thinking about doing it and actually doing it seemed as wide as the Mississippi River.

I fully expected my first book would be about technical matters such as software engineering or the telecommunications industry. Those are the issues that daily fill my professional life.

Instead, here I am writing about a life-changing event that happened to my wife and me. This book is born from an excruciatingly painful period in our lives that God has used and continues to use to bless us as well as to bless others. I hope through my writing about it, this book will bless you and others, too.

At a very young age my wife suffered a stroke, which has left her disabled. However, this unfortunate event has turned out to be a blessing to my family and me. My motivation in sharing this story with you is to provide personal insight on a catastrophic happening in our lives. Mostly, I wish to provide guidance and insight to others who may face a similar fate. Consequently, this book is about the struggle of stroke victims and their families, faith, politics, and hope.

I hope my message is clear: almost anyone at any age in the U.S. can suffer a stroke. Many stroke victims never achieve their potential because of economics or the lack of knowledge of treatments that are available.

I personally hope to be a catalyst who will one day help change the treatment of stroke victims—the 750,000 Americans who each year suffer a stroke. Many of these strokes are preventable. Once a person has a stroke, he or she should not be forgotten by any of us. As a Christian, I also believe I can't emphasize enough the role that prayer and faith in Jesus Christ play in the recovery of stroke victims, their friends, and their families. If you do not know Jesus as your savior, understand that He died so that your sins may be forgiven and that He rose again. He lives today; His grace and forgiveness will open the door for you to everlasting life.

This book is also a call to action. Most of us know someone who has had a stroke; as we get older, most of us have a high probability of having a stroke. All of us are responsible for getting our local, state, and federal governments to act on new legislation that will impact the success of stroke prevention and treatment.

Introduction

My name is Timothy Lee Culver. I am known as Tim. I have written this book in the first person because it is my personal story. I did not suffer a stroke; my wife did. This happened early in our marriage.

I write so you will know hope exists in situations such as the one my wife and I faced. I strongly encourage you to share this book with anyone you know who has had or who knows someone who has had a stroke. Just as important, the message in this book can be applied to any personal tragedy or catastrophic event that occurs in anyone's life.

To understand *Sara's Story*, I need to provide you with some background on my family prior to the stroke. Sara's brother and I were roommates at Baylor University in Waco, TX. Through my future brother-in-law, while I attended Baylor I met Sara. I dated other women but quickly became impressed with Sara. At the time she was rearing her 2-year-old son on her own. She also was attending Baylor on a program that enabled her to simultaneously obtain her Bachelor of Science and Master of Science degrees in mathematics. Over time we developed a friendship, which eventually turned into a full "I-am-in-love-with-you" event. That she actually married me still boggles my mind! I was the guy who did not want to get married and only wanted to see the world. My plans were to marry at about age 30. Instead, I realized that I wanted to spend the rest of my life with Sara. She was absolutely beautiful. She also was the smartest woman I had ever met. I decided I couldn't go through life without her, so I proposed. We were married on December 28, 1985.

In a short amount of space, I can only summarize briefly the next 19 years. In addition to my stepson (who proudly serves with the U.S. Army in Iraq), Sara and I have three children together—Tiffany, 18; Tricia, 15; and Jeremy, 12. Sara completed her education at Baylor and went on to obtain her Master of Science degree in statistics from Southern Methodist University in Dallas, TX. When I met her, Sara had a passion for teaching mathematics. Truthfully, the only reason I obtained a 4.0 grade-point average when I completed my Master of Science degree in the School of Engineering and Applied Science at Southern Methodist University was Sara's help with calculus!

Despite her career interests, Sara believed she needed to stay at home with our small children. I agreed, but it did create a financial strain. Despite staying at home with the children, Sara did manage from 1991 to 2004 to work her schedule so that she could teach mathematics and tutor in the Learning Assistance Center at Eastfield Junior College in Mesquite, TX, near where we lived. Sara loved to teach and certainly wasn't in it for the money!

Sara returned home with stories that displayed her passion. Once she was able to teach a grandmother to add negative numbers. Other times she arrived home just as exuberant about one of her calculus students being accepted to a four-year college. Sara was probably the most dedicated teacher I ever have known. She literally would do anything to help her students. That is probably why she continued in the tutoring program when she easily could have just taught mathematics. She was always excited about any student she could help with mathematics. Sara worked part-time for Eastfield College. She hoped to obtain a full-time position in the fall of 2004. Faculty positions had started to open up; everyone thought that she was a shoe-in for one of them.

Another side of Sara many people in Mesquite knew about was her community involvement. For many years I had played soccer and even coached a men's team. One day my older daughter's coach left the team. My wife asked me to step in and coach. I told her "You have to be kidding. Little kids? No way!" Well, you know who won that argument! I started working with kids. I soon found I had a passion for teaching them soccer, too. I even went on to get my national coaching "C" license and national youth license from U.S. Soccer. I also became involved in the local soccer association and eventually was elected league commissioner. As time passed, the time demands of my soccer involvement conflicted with my escalating responsibilities at work. Something had to give. Much to my surprise Sara wanted to be the league commissioner. She was already doing most of the work anyway, so she was soundly elected to become league commissioner of Mesquite Soccer and succeeded me in the job. This is a tough position. When I first started, Mesquite had 1,100 kids playing soccer. When Sara took over the position, the number had grown to about 3,300. Not only was Sara the league commissioner, but we also had three children now playing soccer.

When the technology downturn occurred in the late 1990s and early 2000, telecommunications spiraled downward. Because I was a director at a company that was on the verge of filing bankruptcy, I knew that I would most likely have to move away from Dallas to find a job. Many of my co-workers and peers had lost their jobs and had discovered no jobs were to be found in the Dallas area. Sara and I discussed our moving or my taking a consulting job and traveling. Sara had established herself in the community; the kids were grounded in their schools, so we made the decision that I would travel to maintain our standard of living. One director I knew had been out of a job almost a year after being laid off. I was determined not to let that happen to me, so I proactively reached out and found a job as a lead telecommunications consultant. From 2001 through July 2004 I traveled Asia, North America, Latin America, the Caribbean, and Europe. My work often took me out of the country for one to two weeks and then back in the country for one week. While this was tough on Sara, my parents lived in the same town as we did and were able to help her extensively.

I must admit that travel did have its perks. Our family took several overseas vacations. In fact, at one point all my children were *Gold* on American Airlines' frequent-flyer program. We even celebrated Thanksgiving in London in 2003. However, that wasn't without a price: we couldn't find any place there that served turkey and dressing!

Church and the Christianity are important to our family. Sara and I were both committed to rearing our children in the Christian faith. Early on we placed them in a Christian school for kindergarten and the first few years of elementary school. We wanted the school to reinforce the Christian values we practiced at home and at church. Our family attended Robinwood Baptist Church in Seagoville, TX, because it was a small church and had a Christian school. The church was not convenient for us, but we went there because the children were in school at Robinwood Christian School. Sadly, the church decided to close down its school because it was a huge financial drain on the church. Our oldest daughter, Tiffany, had attended First Baptist Church of Sunnyvale, TX. She wanted us to try that church. I had reservations because FBC Sunnyvale was huge. I thought I would get lost in the crowd. The first Sunday that we attended, all three kids returned home saying, "I want to join that church." Since the church had six Sunday-school classes in our age group, I told Sara that we should visit each one before we made a decision. I jokingly said that the one that had the best coffee and donuts would win me over. If you know much about Southern Baptists today, you know what I mean! The second Sunday we visited FBC Sunnyvale, we ran into the McClure family. My youngest son and the McClures' oldest were on the same soccer team. We attended Sunday school with them, met one of the best Sunday-school teachers in the world (Bryan Wendt), and ended up joining the church. As usual, Sara quickly started getting active in the church.

I'm sure you realize this introduction provides the background on a family with a "super-mom." The term "super-mom" describes Sara. She took care of the kids, her husband, taught at the local college, volunteered with the local soccer association and parks department, and volunteered at church. At 42, Sara was involved in everything. Almost each hour of each day was orchestrated and planned. How could she do it all—shuttle three kids between soccer practices, keep the house, cook, clean, volunteer, and teach simultaneously?

At 42, Sara was pushing herself to the limit and sacrificing herself for the sake of the children and the community.

Chapter 1

The News

Twelve days after my wife, Sara, suffered a major stroke, the reality of what was really happening began to soak into my head and to touch me on the deepest levels. Until then my usual everything-is-going-to-be-just-fine optimism and strong ability to deal with matters mostly on the cerebral level—paying attention to details and making sure everything was thoroughly organized and done right—carried me along.

Something about the frankness of the words Sara's rehab doctor spoke shook me to my very core and made me face squarely the reality that Sara would never be the same again and that our young lives had taken a turn that we neither one ever could have imagined.

But that's jumping 12 days into this story. Let me start at the beginning when we were just your typical American family living in a suburb, rearing our four children, and doing the things most young couples our age do.

Like so many days in our lives back then, I was on a business trip and Sara was . . . well, as Sara and I always were . . . juggling too many things all at one time.

****

Between January and May 2004, I made nine trips to Europe. I had two projects under way in the United Kingdom, one in Spain, one in Italy, and one prospect in Switzerland. In March 2004 Sara traveled to Switzerland to meet me while I was on a business trip. This was a "getaway" since the kids were not with her. In April 2004 I was working at Telecom Italia. Sara had always wanted to visit Rome, so I promised her that we would go there in May.

Then on May 5, I was in the U.S. and made a one-day trip to Kansas City to visit a prospective project. I took a mid-morning flight, checked into the hotel room, and caught up with the manager over a project I had going with Sprint. We had a short meeting and left for dinner. While I was enroute to the one of Kansas City's famous steak houses, Sara called. She was upset because a rock from a dump truck put a small crack in her windshield. I told her that it wasn't any big deal and that I would get it fixed the next day. Sara said she was still angry about it but was on her way to a parks-board meeting for the City of Mesquite; the board was studying the design of a new park. I told her I loved her. She told me that she loved me, too. Sara said Tiffany was watching the other kids at the house and that she would be back home soon.

I got off the phone and went into the restaurant with Tom Ferry, who was running several projects for me; this included the one at Sprint. Tom was one of those rare individuals you meet on whom you can look back and say with certainty that working with them was one of the highlights of your career. He was extremely ethical and competent. In preparation for the meeting with Dennis, the project sponsor at Sprint, Tom informed me that Dennis was a tentmaker preacher who worked at Sprint full time but also on the side led a large Baptist congregation. I thought to myself, "This is great! I already like this guy."

Tom, Dennis, and I arrived at the restaurant and sat down to order our food. We engaged in small talk. Dennis told me about his ministry and how Sprint was stepping up to help with programs for the local Kansas City community. I was duly impressed. I ordered my meal and was patiently awaiting that famous Kansas City steak when my cell phone rang. On the screen was a Dallas number I didn't recognize. I decided to take the call since I knew my older daughter was watching my 10- and 7-year olds while my wife was at the parks-board meeting.

The call was from James Provence, director of aquatics and sports for the City of Mesquite. The thought of the conversation that followed still brings tears to my eyes because it changed my life forever—at first for the worst and later for the better. The best way to describe this call is just to go through the dialogue.

"Hello." I said.

"Tim Culver?" James asked.

"Yes," I replied

"Tim, this is James," James responded. I recognized his voice since I had worked with him for four years when I was league commissioner

"Hey, James, how's it going?" I asked.

"Tim, your wife, Sara, has had a stroke," said James.

"A stroke? James, are you talking about my mom?" I asked in disbelief.

"No, Sara. She has had a stroke. The paramedics are working on her right now," said James.

"James, a stroke? You are talking about my mom, Billie," I replied.

"No, Tim. It is your wife, Sara. The paramedics are telling me she had a stroke," James said.

"James, what are they going to do with her?" I asked.

"They indicated that they have stabilized her and will be transporting her to Baylor."

"James, thank you. I'm calling my parents to help." I said

in desperation as the reality of what had just happened began to settle into my disbelieving mind.

At this point, all I knew was that something was dreadfully wrong. I kept saying to myself *A stroke? Sara is too young to have a stroke.*

I knew I had to get back to Dallas immediately. Both Dennis and Tom were staring at me. I tried as calmly as possible to tell them what had happened. I explained that my wife was at a parks-board meeting and that the director over athletics and aquatics had just told me Sara had suffered a stroke. I said I needed to get back to Dallas.

By this point my mind was going in 100 different directions at one time. Dennis calmly said, "Let's pray."

I felt fortunate to be with a fellow Christian who could help me regain my focus. At times of such desperation, few men have had the opportunity to have people like Dennis and Tom to support them. We prayed. Tom told me that we needed to go to the hotel to get my belongings so I could head to the airport for my trip back to Dallas. Dennis gave up his meal and offered to help.

On the way to the hotel, all I could think about was getting to Sara. Fortunately I did have enough wits about me to call my parents. I reached my father and explained the situation. I knew he would get the children and take care of them. My mission was to get back to Dallas to be with Sara.

On the way to the Marriott, I called American Airlines. The Executive Platinum desk worked diligently with me on the phone, but things didn't look good for me to make the last flight from Kansas City back to Dallas that night. I couldn't have asked for more support than I received from the woman staffing the phone line.

Dennis and Tom continued to accompany me to take care

of the details. Tom went to the front desk of the Marriott and explained what was happening while I went to my room to pack. When I got to the front desk, the clerk said, "Go, get home to be with your wife!" I asked about the bill and the clerk replied, "Don't worry about that; we have you covered." Tom later explained that the Marriott waived the hotel-room bill. In all my stays at that chain, I have always been impressed that they allow a copy of the Gideon Bible in each hotel room. That night I was impressed with how they treat their customers in a time of crisis.

Dennis and Tom took me to the Kansas City airport as quickly as possible. Fortunately, I wasn't in time to make the flight back to Dallas. Fortunately? Yes, fortunately. God had a better plan for me that evening.

I was determined to get back to Dallas to be with my wife. My father had called to tell me he and my mom would take care of the kids, so Sara was my singular focus. Without another flight out of Kansas City, I had no choice but to drive.

Hertz, the rental-car company, was there to help. Dennis and Tom left me at the Hertz counter. I was able to get a rental car to Dallas. I even got their "Never Get Lost (GPS) system." This turned out to be a good move. Driving in the middle of the night between Kansas City and Dallas offers some of the most desolate stretches of highway on this overpopulated planet.

At the Hertz counter Dennis prayed for me; then I left on my journey.

I could not even begin to tell you the route that I took out of Kansas City. I called my oldest daughter, Tiffany, and told her, "Tiffany, your mother is sick. Mimi and Granddad are on the way to pick up you, Tricia, and Jeremy. You will be staying with them. Pack clothes for them and don't scare them about your mom. I am on the way home. I'll call you guys later." Tiffany is extremely mature and dealt with the situation very well. I then called my father and told him to go ahead and pick up the kids.

Later my mother called me on my cell phone. She told me I should not drive all night. I also called my mother-in-law, who told me that whatever happened, I needed to be careful because she wanted the kids to have at least one parent left. Her words were sobering. I decided I wasn't going to take any chances. I had a mission to get to Dallas, but I vowed not to get killed in the process. I had three children at home depending on me.

As I left Kansas City and headed into the abyss, I started to pray. I had hours ahead of me. In my younger days I probably would have turned on the radio to keep my mind occupied. Fortunately, in recent years I had matured as a Christian. After momentarily turning on the radio, I turned it off. Then in the silence of the road noise I prayed. Despite an occasional phrase such as "left turn is approaching in one mile" from "Never Get Lost" (GPS), I was alone with only God. In retrospect, the fear of driving the distance between Kansas City and Dallas with no chance for sleep was disconcerting. I started praying for Sara. A huge peace that I will never be able to explain fell over me. I never tired and drove the entire seven-hour drive without a problem.

Along the way I had a couple of phone conversations with my father. He told me some facts about Sara's condition. First, he indicated he had been to Baylor Hospital Emergency Room and had found Sara stabilized. He told me her blood pressure in the ER was 240 over 170. Next, he told me that an "old" doctor in the ER had told him Sara would recover and teach again. This gave me hope. I asked my father about the stroke. He explained in layman's terms that it was hemorrhagic stroke. I noted that I was not a doctor and had no idea what that meant. He then explained it as like an aneurism. At that point, I told my father thanks and dropped the phone in panic.

All I could think about was Kaitlynd Phillips, a child who played on a soccer team I had coached. Kaitlynd was a great player and had a very supportive family. She was about 6-years old at the time. I recalled Kaitlynd being at one practice with her mom, who was full of life. The young mother was obviously very proud of her daughter. That Thursday evening Kaitlynd's mom watched from the sidelines. On Saturday Kaitlynd and her mom did not show up for the game. Her mom, about 26, had suffered an aneurysm and died suddenly. This death had really bothered me. I knew the father and could not imagine what he was going through. Even as a Christian I believed no way existed for me to empathize or understand what that family was experiencing. Obviously I no longer have that problem. Today I feel that I could witness and conduct a supportive conversation with anyone.

As I proceeded on my journey to Dallas, I prayed. I knew from Dad's report that the situation was really bad, so I prayed simply that Sara would survive. I asked God to help her survive.

I do not know of many people who have had the opportunity to truly pray. When you have several hours of solitude right after facing a tragedy, you get really close to God. If I had been in Dallas at the time, I would have been caught up in the spiral of activities including getting the kids' stuff packed and rushing to the emergency room. The activities would have distracted me from something that turned out to be very important that night. As I drove, few distractions occurred. At points along the drive no lights shown for miles.

I've known people to face tragedy and say, "Why me?" Some even become angry with God for their predicament. I was more focused on just praying that God would keep my wife alive, because I knew aneurisms are often fatal. My second prayer was a request as follows: "Jesus, help me understand what you want me to learn from this. I need your help and guidance to learn what your plans are and what you want me to learn. Please lift me up and provide guidance. In Jesus' name, I pray." For some reason I never became angry. I totally focused on praying for Sara to survive and for me to understand what God wanted me to learn from this situation.

During the night, I spoke again with my mother-in-law. She was catching a flight to Dallas from Northern Virginia and would meet me the next morning at Baylor Hospital's ICU.

As the sun rose, I inched closer to Dallas. I had been awake all night. I felt a solitude that I had never sensed previously. I felt as though I had gone through a marathon prayer session in which Jesus had prepared me to face the future. Without this preparation my mind would have gone in 100 different directions. Without God's help I know I would not have dealt with the situation very well. You have to understand that I am somewhat impatient and always want to "fix things." I have heard that is a male trait. Instead of my worrying about the next steps, what the doctors were doing, and what I needed to do to fix the problem, God's plan was to provide me the time to get ready to face the tragedy maturely. I arrived at Baylor ICU tired but prepared to face the inevitable—whatever that was.

Chapter 2

Ten Days

After the all-night drive from St. Louis to Dallas' Baylor Hospital ICU, I arrived the morning of May 6, 2004, in remarkably good shape, considering the circumstances. Awake, coherent and rested, I called my mother to let her know her worst fears were not realized. I had not run off some desolate road because of lack of sleep.

My father was at the hospital watching over Sara and awaiting my arrival. I took over the vigil so he could go home. Hospital rules allowed only one family member to be present in the ICU.

When I entered the ICU, I got my first glimpse of Sara. Attached to her were monitors and tubes including IV's. She appeared lifeless. She looked as if she was being kept alive artificially. This was an eerie sight for me, since I had never been exposed to a stroke victim. Most disheartening, her blood pressure was still extremely high. I couldn't understand why it hadn't gone down. Her doctors explained they did not want to throw her body into shock. They also told me that the stroke had affected the right side of her body.

Baylor's ICU was the friendliest ICU I could imagine. Sara's room was equipped not only for her needs but also for her family's. It included a chair that converted into a bed for guests and a desk with high-speed Internet access. I thought being able to dial up the Internet and email friends and relatives on Sara's status was amazing. (Those who know me well and my tendency toward "geek" things were surprised to learn that on my arrival at the hospital I was so concerned about Sarah that I ran off and left my laptop in the car.)

After sitting beside Sara for a period of time, she temporarily regained some amount of consciousness. She could not speak, but I knew from the nurses that she probably could hear somewhat. I told her the kids were with my parents and her mom was on the way. She seemed to smile after I told her that her mom would soon arrive. Sara actually squeezed my hand with her right hand. I falsely jumped to the conclusion that she would recover quickly. Apparently, the affected area of the brain was still functioning. I feel perplexed even today when I recall that the day after the stroke she could squeeze my hand but several days later couldn't do that again with that same right hand.

Soon Sara's mother, Joan Smith, arrived from Virginia. My father picked her up at the airport and brought her straight to the hospital. After she arrived, I went to my parents' home for some needed rest. The kids had stayed home from school that day. I reassured them that their mom would be OK. I told them that she was sick and in the hospital. In truth I had no idea what lay ahead for Sara and all of us.

Little boys are often reared with the admonition not to cry. We men usually believe we are to stand steady and be that reassuring presence for our families. I certainly wanted to maintain this façade with my children. I did not want them to become distressed about their mom. All my bravado was challenged when my youngest son, Jeremy, then 7-years old and four days, woke up from a nap on his grandma's couch and asked for his mom. I struggled to maintain my composure and avoid a complete meltdown in front of the kids. I was able to mutter, "Your mom is sick and at the hospital. Dad is here." Telling a teen-age son about a situation like this is one thing, but having to face a young 7-year old son is quite a different matter altogether.

I returned to the hospital every day. Sara's oldest son, Joshua, and her mother, Joan, traded off shifts with me. They were with her when I was not able to be there. Since Sara seemed to sleep 97 percent of the time, I logged on to my computer and organized everything. I sent e-mails to my employer at the time. Dave Nelson, the CEO of the software company where I worked, offered a long-term, paid leave-of-absence. This was typical for Dave. He was the most ethical and caring person for whom anyone could work. I replied that I would take off only a week because I felt that this was going to be a long-term situation and I would need to take him up on this offer later (as Sara recovered). At one point the hospital staff discussed sending Sara to Baylor's rehabilitation center—once again raising false hopes in me that this would be a quick recovery.

By this point Joan was able to care for our children at our home so they could have as much normalcy in their lives as possible. With Joan, my parents, and me all working together, the children were quickly back attending school and soccer practice. In addition, one of the soccer moms on Tiffany's team volunteered to get Tiffany to and from her practices and games. At least we were able to establish a routine for caring for the children!

With my parents staying with Sara and Joan running the household, I was able to work some.

I notified my church to enlist prayer support. Instead of just praying, members pitched in with some much-needed help. Our Sunday Bible class started to bring a meal each evening. They continued to do this for three months! I remember fondly how I gained 15 pounds because that class has some of the best cooks in Dallas!

The days seemed to be going by more and more slowly.

The doctors arrived and ran test after test. After Sara had been in the ICU for a week, her blood pressure remained extremely high. My "fix it" male syndrome kept kicking in. I kept thinking to my self, "Why don't these doctors just lower the blood pressure? Surely they've got some medication that will do that." After a couple of days in the ICU Sara no longer squeezed my hand. I kept feeling that her high blood pressure was continuing to damage her. This turned out to be my worst-case scenario. The doctors seemed obsessed with finding out why her blood pressure had shot through the roof. After eight or nine days of testing her, they finally concluded she simply had high-blood pressure.

About the eighth day in ICU an administrator-type person, although courteous, visited to tell us that Baylor's rehabilitation center was full, so they were looking at moving Sara to some other location. This would have added 45 minutes to our commute to visit her. I had done some preliminary research and found that Baylor Rehabilitation was one of the top units of its type in the country. Sara's mom and I prayed that God would open the door to get Sara into Baylor Rehabilitation. Sara's mom even started an email chain asking people to pray for Sara to be placed in Baylor Rehabilitation.

The doctors told me a feeding tube was nourishing Sara. They told me many stroke victims have to relearn to swallow as well as to chew. Seeing this tube in her mouth every day was disturbing. Nevertheless, I remained hopeful. As I've already illustrated many times in this book, that's just part of my personality.

Finally, a doctor who specializes in swallowing—until then I had never known of such a specialty—took Sara for x-rays. He determined that her caregivers could start trying to give her some solid foods. She still could not have certain types of food that might make her choke. Once again I saw this announcement as yet another glimmer of hope. I watched Sara swallow food. I believed this was a good sign, although I did note she had to be reminded to swallow.

Sara had been teaching three classes at Eastfield Community College. I found all of her materials and pulled the grades together and delivered them to the mathematics department. I knew that Sara would want me to insure that the students were taken care of while she was in the hospital. Final grades were to be posted soon; I knew Sara took her responsibility for that very seriously. When I told Sara that I had done this for her, she managed a small semblance of a smile.

On Sara's ninth day in the ICU a hospital administrator popped in to tell me that a bed had opened up at Baylor Rehabilitation. Our prayers had been answered! This was the first in a series of emotional ups and downs that our family would go through during this ordeal. Joan and I were on top of the world. We could see a path to recovery.

My wife was on her way to Baylor Rehabilitation. On the day of the big move from ICU to Baylor Rehabilitation, I expected the hospital to wheel her across the street. Instead, I was fascinated to learn that Baylor had built an underground tunnel system to connect its various hospitals.

Sara now was on her way to Baylor Rehabilitation. I was exuberant. Economist Alan Greenspan had just used this term in referring to market behavior in the past, so I now knew what it meant.

Chapter 3

Devastation

At Baylor Rehab Sara was placed on the third floor in a room with eight other people. For those individuals that need constant monitoring, Baylor Rehab has special rooms in which a nursing staff monitors them 24 hours, seven days a week. I have never been hospitalized and have had few friends or family members in the hospital; so all this was new to me. Consequently this was a scene I was not prepared to experience.

I looked around the room and realized that each person had a story. A man across the room had bought four-wheelers for himself and his son. In their first outing he flipped his four-wheeler and was completely paralyzed except that he could still talk. I couldn't imagine the suffering that family was going through. Nearby was a fellow who while working had a box drop on him—paralyzing him from the waist down. This guy was "quite a trip", if you know what I mean. He asked if my wife had been in an auto accident. I replied *no*. He told me, "I have a great lawyer. I have his cards to pass out right here." I found unbelievable the fact that in the rehabilitation center I had run across an ambulance chaser. I looked around and realized how lucky I was that Sara would recover.

The second day in Baylor Rehab, Sara said a word to me. She said, "Love you". I could not believe it. I was completely overwhelmed with joy. Sara could speak. Right there in the room I broke down and cried. I said prayers of thanks.

Soon I had to go home so I could work. I was very fortunate that I could work from home and keep up with everything. Joan also was a Godsend. I wish everyone could have a mother-in-law like she is. I had never really gotten to know Joan that well because of the geographical distance. My mother was scheduled for hip-replacement surgery and could not do much to help. She decided to hire someone to clean up our house and assist Joan. Things were getting organized! While things were not normal, we were settling into a routine. Sara was at Baylor Rehab, the kids were back on their schedules, we were receiving support from our church, and the future looked bright—or so I thought.

My optimism was soon shattered when I received that call from Dr. Porter, to whom I referred in the opening of chapter 1. He was in charge of Baylor Rehab and was my wife's doctor. He began our conversation with his recommendations that Sara be transferred to Baylor's long-term, acute-care facility. Dumfounded, I asked why. Dr. Porter advised that Sara needed to recover more before going through rehab. He explained that my insurance coverage for rehabilitation was very limited. Further, he indicated that she could take only an hour of rehabilitation a day and that her best interests were to utilize Baylor Rehabilitation when doing so would benefit her the most. His words burst my bubble. Joan was visiting Sara at rehab, the kids were at school, and I was at home working alone. As the seriousness of the situation soaked further into my analytical, optimistic brain, I felt so terribly afraid for my wife, our children, and, yes, for myself, too. *What did all of this mean?* I wondered.

I have a lot of respect for Dr. Porter. He is very articulate and extremely good at what he does. I decided to probe further. Dr. Porter explained to me that Sara suffered from acute aphasia and that the stroke had done considerable damage to her brain. I then mentioned what the "old doctor" had told my dad in the ER and that Sara had squeezed my hand the day after the stroke. That's when Dr. Porter gave me a reality check. Of course, I asked for it. I told Dr. Porter that I was accustomed to dealing bluntly with professionals. I explained that I needed to know facts, prognosis, etc. I told him that was how I operated.

Dr. Porter proceeded to tell me that Sara had suffered an acute stroke. He indicated that he doesn't normally treat people that have had a stroke as severe as Sara's because they don't survive.

"What?" I said. "They don't survive?"

"No," he replied. "No, Tim they don't survive."

I then said, "Dr. Porter, give it to me straight. What is her prognosis?"

He replied, "Tim, Sara will never walk, talk, or interact with people again. That is what I can tell you at this time."

I felt like I had just been run over by a freight train! My mind was going 90-miles per hour.

Dr. Porter asked, "Are you OK?"

I replied, "Yes, I think so. Give me a second."

He then replied, "I know this is tough, but these are the preliminary findings. Let's get her over to the long-term care facility for four weeks so we can reassess her ability to go through the program here at Baylor Rehabilitation. We can also reassess her long-term prognosis."

I was devastated. The reality of the seriousness of the situation had finally soaked to the very core of my being. No one was at the home, so I was all by myself. For at least two hours I cried and prayed. Throughout the past 12 days I had gone through emotional ups and downs and had convinced myself everything was going well. Now my legs had been knocked right out from under me. I prayed that the situation Dr. Porter described would not be true. I asked Jesus to lift me up and give me hope.

When Joan arrived home, I told her what had happened. We both cried. I told her that all I wanted Sara to be able to do was at least talk, so that she could tell me how she feels and if she needs anything. I told Joan that I had prayed that I didn't care about her physical abilities at this point. I just wanted to be able to understand what she wanted so I could comfort her.

Fortunately, Joan and I both were sufficiently recovered to not alarm the children when they arrived home from school.

Both Joan and I reached out to others to ask them to pray for Sara. My mind also flashed back to the man in the hospital ward who was a paraplegic but could talk. I started thinking how lucky his family was that he could at least talk to those caring for him and tell them what he needed.

Inside of me emotionally a 180-degree shift was beginning to occur. I did continue down the path of not opening up to the kids and explaining to them what was really happening. Part of this was because of my concerns about their ability to deal with the bottom line about their mom. Truthfully, the other part was because I was an emotional wreck and wanted to remain strong in front of them. I knew I could not tell the kids the truth about their mom without my breaking down. As I write this from my recollections of the events of those days, I am still emotional; tears flood my eyes.

As the day wore on, I eventually was tired enough to sleep. Before I went to sleep, I prayed for guidance. My prayer went something like this, "Jesus, I am desperate. I have no clue what to do next. I need your help and guidance. I know you want me to learn something from this. Please help me find that meaning. Please help provide me guidance on what I need to do."

The next morning when I awoke, I knew I had a mission. Somehow, God had revealed to me not to give up. This was not revealed to me in a dream; it was more of a sensation and sense that fell over me. I know that this may sound weird to some, but you would have had to experience it yourself to understand. All I can say is that prayers were answered. I was a new man and more determined than ever to confront the situation head on and honestly. I now believed I was on God's side in this battle for my family's future and that He was on my side, too. I left the house with a mission to help move Sara from Baylor Rehab to the Baylor long-term, acute-care facility. I vowed not to give in or give up. I was ready to challenge any doctor or any institution that got in Sara's way.

Another encouragement arrived in the form of a note to Sara from American Airlines. I had a backlog of mail in the mailbox. I noticed a card addressed to Sara Culver, so I opened it. The card was from the Executive Platinum Desk at American Airlines. It was not a "company official" letter with the AA logo but a simple get-well card to Sara. Whoever was working the desk the night I called in desperation looking for a flight back to Dallas had taken a moment to buy and send the card. The person had 40 people working the Executive Platinum Desk sign the card. She even wrote a note wishing Sara the best and said those signing the card were also praying for her recovery. I sat in shock as tears welled up in my eyes as I thought about someone I only knew through a phone conversation who had been touched enough to do this for Sara and me. The next day I wrote a letter to American Airlines' CEO telling him about the card and how much I appreciated it! I asked him to personally thank the Executive Platinum desk on my behalf.

Chapter 4

Long-term Acute Care

Joan and I loaded up Sara's flowers, teddy bears, and other items people had sent to her and carted them to Sara's new home on the second floor of the Baylor Long-term Acute Care Hospital on Gaston Avenue in Dallas. The hospital staff had assured me Sara would continue to receive as much rehabilitation there as she could endure.

Sara slept most of the time. Later I learned that a severe brain injury requires a substantial amount of rest. Without her intravenous medicine, feeding tubes, and other items that by now had been discontinued, Sara appeared more normal. Joan and I opted to start taking the kids to see their mom on a regular basis. At first, the kids were a little taken aback with Sara's condition. That made me very glad they did not see her initially. I knew her earlier tubes, ports, and medical machinery would have frightened them severely. I did not want Sara's condition to damage them any more than they already had been by the trauma.

The hospital staff was very supportive of our children visiting with their mother. I personally believed that Sara needed to see the kids, too. I believed her motherly instincts would rise up to help her overcome the odds against her. We settled into a routine and visited on a regular basis. However, every so often we added some spice to the mix. Once I spoke with a nurse about possibly bringing Pepper, our puppy, to visit Sara. I explained how Sara had really taken a shine to the 2-month-old dog. We wrapped Pepper in a coat and walked down the hall. Another nurse saw us and was not pleased! I explained that another nurse had said our bringing Pepper to the hospital was OK. (Secretly I hoped I didn't get the first nurse in trouble). When we walked into the room with Pepper, Sara lit up like I had never seen in long time and exclaimed, "Wow!" On her face was a smile that was unbelievable. As we spoke with her, we found out that she was really surprised at how big Pepper had gotten. That was the reason for the *Wow!*

Over the course of three or four weeks I personally had observed Sara becoming a little more alert each day. Her stamina seemed to be picking up, too. She had no use of her right leg or arm, but I could see her personality returning. Having by this point been on the emotional roller coaster, I had developed a guarded optimism. At the same time I kept reflecting back on that sensation which I received after praying for guidance—that I should not give up.

On the four-week anniversary of Sara's stroke, Dr. Porter evaluated Sara and indicated that she was making progress. However, he said she needed a couple of more weeks at the long-term acute-care facility. That was my "Wow!"—a positive report from Dr. Porter! Things were beginning to look up!

Meanwhile at the Culver household things were changing. My mother-in-law is the most organized person I have ever known. She cannot stand for a home to be in disarray. She says that everything goes more smoothly when in order. The Scripture *Let everything be done decently and in order* (1 Cor. 14:40) seemed to be her motto. The bar had definitely been raised for the kids and for me!

The kids had to keep their rooms neat. No toys were to be left downstairs. Even my tools were subject to the new laws of the household. Once when I had replaced the downstairs bathroom doorknob because it wasn't working, I left the screwdriver on the table with the intention of taking it back out to the garage later. When I went downstairs, Joan gave me *that look*. Without her saying a word, *that look* communicated that I had messed up something even though I didn't even realize it. It's *that look* that says, "You should have known better." You feel helpless because you have no clue what you have done wrong. Joan educated me by saying, "We don't leave tools lying on the kitchen table in the house that I am taking care of." I thought to myself, *OK, I thought I had done something really bad. She must have taught that look to Sara.* I smiled and took the screwdriver to the garage.

Other notable changes were occurring in our household, too. For instance, Joan is fantastic at instilling old-fashioned values. In contrast I am a member of the first fast-food generation. At least I was before Joan moved in. Previously I would courteously drop by McDonald's, Arby's, Burger King, or Taco Bell and pick up breakfast, lunch, or dinner for everyone in the family. When I would get home, I would drop the food on the table for the kids to eat—usually quickly because we were late getting back from somewhere such as a soccer practice or late going somewhere such as a soccer game.

Joan was born in the generation where meals for the family were prepared at home and everyone ate together. In Joan's mind that was the way life was supposed to be! In Joan's era the table was meticulously organized including a prayer before each meal. To put it mildly, even though I thought this was quaint and nice, this definitely was not how Sara, our children, and I lived!

At one point I had to go on a quick three-day business trip to Puerto Rico. During that time Joan had been teaching the kids how to properly set the dinner table. I arrive home from Puerto Rico in time for dinner. That's when I definitely noticed the impact Joan was having on our children. I sat down at the table and started to serve myself. I noticed Jeremy (7 at the time) standing behind his chair. I told him to sit down and eat. He responded, "I am waiting for the ladies of the house to sit down first." I felt as though my whole world had suddenly quaked. I felt like a heel. I sincerely appreciated Joan teaching these old-fashioned values to our children.

My generation has a fast-paced lifestyle. We structure every moment of every day. Our kids lead a structured life. We eat fast food and focus on convenience. We do all of this because we have a modern lifestyle and try to cram something into every moment of every day. No wonder so many people are stressed out, so we end up with strokes, cancer, and other ailments because of our hectic lifestyle and food that we eat! Joan certainly helped me face the dark side of all this.

Besides being a wife and a mother Joan had been a school-teacher and a successful real-estate agent. She resigned from her business and concentrated on my household. She and I joked that this was a mixed blessing.

While Sara's time in ICU seemed to drag on as if in slow motion, her time in Baylor Acute Long-term Care seemed to pass entirely too quickly. I believe I observed one of the reasons for this. In the ICU relatives and friends of ill loved ones focus on watching the instruments. We become mesmerized watching all the ICU instruments and keep stressing about our loved one's status. Even on Sara's seventh and eighth days in ICU I recall fixating on the blood pressure monitors and asking over and over, "Why doesn't her blood pressure drop down?"

If I could do things over again, I would channel my feelings of helplessness and lack of knowledge into prayers for Sara, our children, Joan, Welton (Sara's father), my parents, and others. That's what I would advise anyone facing a similar crisis.

Once we were in the acute-care facility time passed quickly. Soon we were beginning the sixth week. That's when I finally received some great news. Dr. Porter had re-tested Sara and determined that she was ready for Baylor Rehabilitation. Our prayers were answered!

Simultaneously a bed became available the Baylor Institute for Rehabilitation. I determined that Sara would go there and improve. I also did not know the determination that Sara had in her to do the same. Later in this book I'll tell you about that. Needless to say I now I count Sara as one of my personal heroes; I respect her for many things but most assuredly her determination and sheer willpower.

The day we had been praying for finally arrived. After six long weeks we moved Sara to Baylor Rehabilitation.

Chapter 5

Baylor Rehabilitation

Sara returned to the same rehab hospital room in which she originally stayed. The feeling truly was one of *déjà vu*. Our positive feelings were clouded by the sad fact that the faces of the other patients had all changed.

I looked around the room and spotted a young man who was about 17. He had not been there previously. His parents tirelessly looked after him. I could see the desperation in their eyes and their need for hope. I tried to strike up a conversation, but the parents were not ready to talk yet.

The young man I called "The Gangster" was now gone, too. I'm sure his lawyer got a good settlement for him.

I looked around in amazement at the other people who worked in this place. Day in and day out they cared for the patients and kept such a positive attitude. One middle-aged woman working there said "Miss Sara, welcome back." Sara smiled. The people working at Baylor Rehabilitation amazed me with their thoughtful expressions such as this!

I questioned Sara being in a group setting with eight to 10 other people requiring 24/7 monitoring. Baylor personnel responded that they were looking for a permanent room for her. Within a day or two Sara had her own room. This amazed me, since my insurance only covered a semi-private room. Dr. Porter apparently believed that to recover, Sara needed to be able to focus without other people distracting her. I did not know it at the time, but when a person is recovering from a brain injury, everything distracts him or her.

When Sara re-entered Baylor Rehabilitation, she wasn't in any better condition than when she had left weeks earlier. However, she was awake more often and seemed more mentally alert. She had received some therapy but nothing intensive while she was in Baylor's long-term, acute-care unit. Sara could not initiate speech; she could not walk or use her right leg and arm; she also was incontinent. Nevertheless Sara had reached a point in which she was aware of her situation. She faced it with incredible courage. In her face and emotions I could see the desire to recover. I knew instinctively she wanted to get well and go home. Sara could not tell me these things, but in my heart I could feel them.

On the home front Joan continued to be a Godsend. She helped with the kids, visited Sara each day, and went to church with me each Sunday. For me the highlight of Sunday school time was reporting on how Sara was doing. Our church had truly adopted my family! Members will never know how much their caring meant to me personally.

After a month or so Joan returned to Virginia for a week. My father-in-law took family leave from his job to replace her. Welton literally drove to the airport in Virginia, met his wife in the terminal, where he kissed her hello and goodbye, then got on a plane bound for Texas. Joan took back home the car in which Welton arrived! They were almost like the proverbial "two ships passing in the night", only their passing occurred deliberately and in the airport! Their routine continued for 10 months until Welton's retirement in March 2005.

At one point Joan's sister, Marcia, who lived in Florida, took a week's vacation so Joan and Welton could have a few days off to be together. Sara's brothers and several other relatives flew to Texas to see and encourage her.

Welton and Joan made extreme sacrifices to help us. For months Welton lived without his wife at home and then gave up his planned retirement home in the mountains of Virginia to move to Texas to care for Sara and our family. Joan practically moved into our home to assist us.

Joan, Welton. my parents, and I made sure our kids saw Sara on a regular basis. I personally believed the children's visits and Sara's desire to be a mother would encourage her to continue to focus on recovery.

Insurance is one of those issues and chores that face most people in situations like ours. For 13 years Sara had been working part-time at Eastfield College. Part-time employees there did not receive benefits. That made me even more thankful for Social Security. Joan's brother was disabled and received Supplemental Social Security, which I saw as encouraging for us. Since Sara had no income now and I had three kids still at home, I knew that the disability coverage would be a great help to the family.

Applying for Social Security turned out to be a laborious task. I am what most people would call *technically savvy*, but I experienced much difficulty with the Social Security Administration's early attempts at automation of the application process. Now streamlined, the system at the point when Sara had her stroke combined some online and some mail-in forms and actions. That combination would confuse anyone of any educational and technical proficiency. I finally was able to fill out the paperwork. Doing so took me 12 hours. Remember, I'm the guy who is supposed to be technically savvy. Twelve hours! The process was frustrating to no end. I made a mental note to contact my congressman to complain. Unfortunately I found out that that Sara did not qualify for any Social Security disability benefits! I was in shock. Sara had elected a state withholding versus Social Security. Since she worked for the county, Social Security assumed the state would provide her with insurance. Unfortunately, at the school at which Sara taught, part-time employees do not get disability insurance.

Meanwhile, Baylor Rehab turned into somewhat of a routine—that is, after I figured out the routine. Periodically Joan or I would attend Sara's OT, PT, or ST classes. If these initials sound like Greek to you, please know that they were truly a foreign language to me, also. OT stands for Occupational Therapy, PT for Physical Therapy, and ST for Speech Therapy. Throughout Sara's rehabilitation process, these initials and what they stood for became extremely important issues for Sara and for me.

Although at first Sara seemed shy, she exhibited an extremely positive mental attitude. She strongly believed she was going to recover. I credit this to her family's support. Sara did not spend a day without someone from her family visiting her. I saw other patients there who had limited family support. I could not imagine being in a place like that without a strong supportive family behind me. I learned that many patients lapse into depression, which exacerbates their problems. Sara would have none of this and quickly became a favorite of the staff. From the orderlies who took her to therapy to the therapists themselves, they all loved Sara's attitude.

Sara and I would go on "dates" at Baylor. I know this sounds corny, but I would order a "to-go" meal at a restaurant and a DVD from Blockbuster. I then would take my laptop to to Sara's room at the hospital. Sara would sit up in bed so we could watch the video together. Though I was very conscious that she was on a restricted diet, I often would share some of my meal with her. With very little activity of any kind, a patient faces gaining weight, which could be detrimental to his or her recovery.

Both Joan and I could see the improvement occurring in Sara while she was at Baylor Rehabilitation. The enthusiasm of the individuals that work in the therapy areas was impressive. Joan was especially impressed with a therapist named Rachel, who told Sara, "You will walk again. You will come back to visit me and walk into Baylor Rehabilitation without a wheelchair."

Rachel also told Joan how much joy she received getting to work with Sara. Many severely ill patients endure bouts of depression. I am certain that I would be one of those people. I would be kicking and screaming and probably be the worst person to deal with. Sara, on the other hand, maintained her positive attitude and determination. In a way, her attitude was an answer to prayer. Instead of depression, what we saw exhibited in Sara was extreme determination that you see in athletes that achieve Olympic gold.

I recall watching Rachel work with Sara as they used two walking bars. Rachel asked Sara whether she was tired and wanted to quit. Sara responded, "go again" and refused to sit down. I had never before seen in Sara this type of determination. Sara had never been athletic or desired to compete in physical activities. Sara's mom had mentioned the same observation. Reflecting back on those days I know Sara's attitude was a direct reaction to the many prayers for her recovery. While individuals may not have prayed specifically for Sara to have this determination and willpower, God knew what she needed and gave it to her. Where else would such sheer willpower and determination originate?

Baylor Rehabilitation was a very unique place. Without a lot of bureaucratic hurdles to cross I was able to take Sara out of her room in her wheelchair. This presented a special opportunity for me to interact with her. Her speech therapist told the family that Sara had severe aphasia, which meant that the area of the brain that controls speech was affected. Sara had to relearn much of the speech that we take for granted. Her behavior was almost as if an index in her brain that pointed to right word choices was corrupted. Sara had problems either finding the right word or using a correct one.

On our dates I would push her wheelchair around the hospital. We enjoyed looking at the hospital's artwork. To help Sara in her recovery I would point out things in a picture. If she had difficulty, I would tell her what the object in the painting was. Sara referred to the paintings as windows. I told her they were *paintings*. In some ways, she was correct. Paintings are windows—but instead of to the outside world, they are insights into the world of the artist.

On Sunday mornings either Joan or I would skip the worship service after Sunday school and go to be with Sara. Baylor Rehabilitation held a Sunday-morning worship service, which Sara wanted to attend. She did not want to be late to it!

One Sunday morning my turn to take Sara to the worship service occurred. I left Joan and the kids at church and headed to the rehab center. I took Sara to the chapel. About that time several other patients also arrived for the service. We all set there and waited . . . and waited . . . and waited! No preacher or lay leader showed up to lead us. Finally, I spoke up and said "Well, I am not a preacher, but I went to Sunday school this morning. I'll be glad to lead a session with all of you. I don't have anything prepared, but we can cover the lesson I had this morning."

At that moment the Holiday Inn Express commercial popped into my mind; that's the one where someone performs brain surgery or stops a nuclear disaster and exclaims confidently something such as "I'm not a doctor (or nuclear physicist or whatever), but I stayed at the Holiday Inn Express last night."

After I made my offer to lead the worship service, an elderly woman said, "go right ahead." In the meantime Sara was punching me in the side saying, "No!" I asked Sara, "Are you afraid I'll embarrass you?" She replied, "Yes!" I told her "I promise I won't embarrass you."

The older woman told Sara, "Let him go ahead", so Sara gave me the go-ahead nod. About halfway through covering our Sunday-school lesson that morning an announcement was heard over the loudspeaker. It stated that the morning worship service was canceled. Toward the end of my "debut" as a preacher an out-of-breath young pastor showed up to apologize for no one being there. The older woman said, "Don't worry, son, we have us a preacher over there"—and she pointed to me. I thought "Wow. I never thought I could have this type of impact." I replied by asking the young preacher, "How much do you get paid for this?" He laughingly replied that we needed to pass the plate. Sara told me I did a good job and smiled. That made my day.

As I mentioned before, in the midst of all this my mother was in need of hip-replacement surgery. Because of Sara's condition Mom tried to put it off as long as possible. However, the pain had grown too much for her. So, my mom had hip-replacement surgery and ended up for therapy in Baylor Rehabilitation afterward. The odds of one's wife and one's mother both being in rehabilitation at the same time and in the same place must be quite small! Sara was thrilled to be able to visit her mother-in-law in the same hospital.

As time passed, Sara's abilities increased. She was getting better in her attempts to walk. Her speech was improving. Her mental awareness and memory were also improving. I was getting really pumped up about her progress.

Being the pragmatist that I am, in the back of my mind I kept thinking about Dr. Porter's comments about the limitations of our insurance coverage for rehabilitation. He earlier told me that after Sara got out of Baylor Rehabilitation, our insurance would only cover about 30 additional outpatient visits.

Despite this dark cloud looming over her upcoming deadline, I continued to see some real progress in Sara's skills. The families of a couple of other patients I befriended impressed this concern about the limitations of our insurance coverage on me even more. The families also had limits in their policies on the time individuals could spend in a hospital. As their limit for rehabilitation drew near, these families worried about their options. I spoke with the family of one woman whose benefits had reached their maximum and was being discharged. She had no outpatient benefits and was going home, where no one was trained to help her. I could envision her actually going backward in her recovery. I did not want this to happen to Sara. I could see the potential of Sara moving beyond where she was at this time. Every night I prayed about my concern. In the first part of my prayer I thanked God for being with us that day and for Sara's progress. In the second part of my prayer I asked for Sara's continued progress and recovery.

The day was approaching when Sara would hit the limit to what the insurance company would cover. My insurance carrier was Highmark Blue Cross Blue Shield of Pennsylvania. To this point the company had provided excellent service. Dr. Porter's assistant, Nikki, told us we needed to start the process of moving to Sara's next phase. When Nikki first made us aware of the transition, I happened to be out of town on a business trip. Joan attended the session. In that conference Baylor Rehabilitation recommended a nursing home and said Sara would need 24/7 care the rest of her life. When Joan told me this, I said, "No way". Instead of cowering to the dictates of an insurance company, I refused to accept this determination. Sara was making progress. I could not accept that she would need 24/7 care for the rest of her life. Early on after the devastating news of the stroke God had empowered me that I was not to give up. No matter what the odds, I was not going to give up on Sara.

I called and spoke with Dr. Porter. I told him I could not accept his conclusion. In all fairness to the staff at Baylor Rehabilitation, they often have to make decisions based on the best outcome for the patient combined with the economics of insurance. The family's ability to shoulder the medical costs certainly weighs in the decision. Dr. Porter was a straight shooter. I liked that. I told him that sending Sara to a nursing home was not acceptable. He told me that this is what the insurance company would cover. He then suggested two other alternatives. These other alternatives were facilities in the Dallas area that treated traumatic brain injuries (TBI). After consulting with Joan, I decided to pursue having representatives from these two facilities visit with Sara. Meanwhile the deadline was looming on Sara's discharge.

Both of the local TBI treatment centers sent representatives to Baylor to visit Sara and to perform evaluations. Joan and I decided to visit each facility. We spent about eight hours visiting each location. One was more geared as a group home; the other provided more individual attention. The Centre for Neuro Skills provided the type of atmosphere that both Joan and I thought would benefit Sara. She was a grown woman with four kids. We just could not picture her in a group home atmosphere. We knew Sara would want her privacy.

Joan and I also watched the therapy in action at these centers. We liked the individual attention we witnessed at CNS. Joan and I both walked away from CNS with the distinct opinion that this is where Sara should be. We informed Baylor about our decision.

As the deadline approached for Sara's discharge, Dr. Porter's assistant indicated that the insurance carrier would not cover Sara for CNS. In addition, Steve Robinson, admissions coordinator for CNS, indicated that things were not going well in terms of their getting Sara admitted. At this point, Nikki gave me a list of nursing homes to visit as options for Sara.

Disappointment filled my thoughts and feelings. I thought, *a nursing home? Not if I can help it!*

Chapter 6

Nursing Home – No Way!

Despite my misgivings I now had a list of 10 nursing homes to visit. At this point, I was starting to doubt myself and the message that I believed God had given me not to give up. Nobody except me and a few other family members believed Sara could ever return to anything like a normal life.

I tried being practical, which is easy for someone with an engineering mindset to do. I told myself, *Sara couldn't take care of herself. Joan can't take care of her by herself. What alternative do we have?*

Yes, Sara had progressed and was making progress. No, she had not recovered to the level that she or I would have liked. Living in the tension was frustrating.

This was one of the reasons I was so bothered to think of her being discharged from Baylor Rehabilitation and sent to a nursing home permanently.

Even worse, I was disturbed by the fact that many individuals who could still make significant progress were being discharged from Baylor because of insurance-company policies. My fight was to save my wife from exile to a nursing home. Yet in the back of my mind I felt sad and angry that these others were being discharged to go home and waste away, too. I told myself that after Sara recovered, I would take up their causes as well.

After telling myself all this, my practical side would emerge and say, *You need to be practical. A nursing home would be a stopgap until you can find a new solution.*

I decided to visit the suggested nursing homes.

Joan was personally familiar with nursing homes because she had taught Bible classes to elderly women, many of whom living in nursing homes. Her own mother-in-law in her later years also had been confined to one. I, however, was not prepared for what I saw in the nursing homes. Walking down the halls of those institutions I saw them as places families put loved ones who have no hope. These were places in which you put people who were too sick to care for at home or for people for which at-home care was too inconvenient. *Too inconvenient* may be harsh because I realize that many people do not have the resources and ability to care for their loved ones at home. But on the inside that is how I described these situations.

I called the insurance company to discuss the issue. The person with whom I spoke told me nursing homes can provide therapy like Sara received at Baylor Rehabilitation and that this could be covered by the insurance policy.

I visited unannounced each of the nursing homes. My impression was that these were not places that a 42-year-old woman should be confined—much less a place where a 70-year old ought to live. To put it mildly, on the emotional level I had a severe allergic reaction to the whole idea of nursing homes.

Then my pragmatic side would kick in also. I could see how putting people unable to care for themselves in a nursing home could be a compassionate act, if no other alternative existed. This did not eradicate my feeling that nursing homes are places in which hope is scarce.

I walked in utter amazement down the halls of the nursing homes I visited. Most of the people there were elderly. I did spot a few people in their 40s and 50s. Most likely were there because of an accident or catastrophic health problem such as a stroke. Regardless whether the person was 40 or 80, I did notice one consistent theme: each lonely person seemed to have a glimmer of hope that I was there to visit them. They were there wasting away in nothingness.

I knew in my heart of hearts that I could never put anyone in my family (my parents, my in-laws, my wife, or my children) into a nursing home—unless doing so was the option of last resort. The looks of despair on the people's faces disturbed me greatly.

I visited three nursing homes on the list of 10. In a couple of them, I spoke with the residents about therapy. I decided that the therapy proposition proposed by the insurance company was a farce. The residents spoke of getting a few hours of therapy a week. Sara was getting at least five hours a day and making slow progress. I could not fathom how cutting back to a few hours a week would benefit her at all.

Despite my initial self-doubts, I firmly believed God did not want me ever to place Sara in a nursing home.

Let me hasten to add: I certainly applaud the caregivers in these nursing homes. However, their objective is to minimize costs and provide subsistence living. My focus was on helping Sara recover and become self-sufficient again. Nursing homes struck me as places to put people "out to pasture with dignity." Sara was 42, had four children (three at home and one on his way to Iraq), and a husband who needed her back at home.

My mind was fully made up: Sara is NOT going to a nursing home.

I went home and discussed the situation with Joan. We both agreed that Sara needed to go to CNS.

But how, oh Lord, how? I asked.

Chapter 7

Taking Risks – The Fight Begins

A representative from Centre for Neuro Skills (CNS) visited Sara in the hospital for the initial evaluation. The evaluator also spent a considerable amount of time poring over Sara's records at Baylor Rehabilitation as well as visiting with staff. As mentioned previously, Joan and I had visited two Dallas-area facilities that treat traumatic brain injuries. The Dallas-Fort Worth Metroplex is fortunate to have two facilities such as these in the area. Many large cities across the country do not have these types of treatment centers. The CNS staff person that evaluated Sara gave a comprehensive report on Sara's current state and indicated belief that CNS could substantially help Sara. Joan and I already knew this instinctively. The next steps were to get my insurance carrier to cover treatment at CNS.

I contacted Steve Robinson, admissions coordinator for CNS, to provide him the insurance information. In addition, we let Baylor Rehabilitation know our intentions of having Sara moved to CNS. Everything seemed to be moving toward our goal, so Joan gave a great report to my Sunday-school class on July 4, 2004, and mentioned our plan. Little did I know the bureaucratic snafus, roadblocks, and difficulties that lay ahead.

On the following Tuesday, Steve Robinson called to let me know he was running into problems with Highmark Blue

Cross Blue Shield. Steve had previously told me that CNS had a contract with Blue Cross Blue Shield, so he believed Sara's admission should not be an issue. As things turned out, CNS had a contract with Blue Cross Blue Shield of Texas! I have had Blue Cross Blue Shield policies for many years and never realized that each one of the Blue Cross Blue Shield (BCBS) companies is a separate organization with separate policies. Even Pennsylvania, where my current employer has its policy, had two separate BCBSs in the state!

The fun and games with insurance bureaucracy was about to move to a new level for me. Things were about to get highly complicated.

BCBS of Texas covered treatment of traumatic brain injuries through an assisted-living facility license. The State of Texas issues assisted-living-facility licenses and medical-care-facility licenses. Nursing homes fall under the medical-care-facility licenses. The State of Texas had regulated that facilities such as CNS should fall under the assisted-living-facility license. Unknown to me, Texas has been very progressive in legislation mandating the coverage of therapy to recover from traumatic brain injuries. Any policy sold or administered in the State of Texas required the carrier to cover therapy. In addition, the legislation specifically put facilities such as CNS under the assisted-living licensing board. Why is all this relevant? Highmark BCBS of Pennsylvania's coverage that was sold to my employer only covered care in a facility licensed as a medical-care facility. Therefore, Highmark BCBS denied the coverage for Sara in CNS. In addition, I later found out from the Texas Department of Insurance that the law didn't even apply to Highmark BCBS because the policy was sold in Pennsylvania! While the intent of the Texas law was commendable, many Texas citizens are not covered because their insurance policies are sold to their employers in another state!

I made a note to myself that this was yet another action for me to pursue after Sara recovered.

Steve Robinson spent a considerable amount of time with the case manager from Highmark BCBS. He reported that he was getting nowhere. He told me things did not look promising. I then told him I would get Sara covered. I actually do not think he believed me. The battle was about to heat up!

I called the case manager at Highmark BCBS. She was completely unfamiliar with traumatic brain injuries or any type of program such as CNS. She told me that CNS was experimental medicine and that I needed to get Sara into a facility that provided medical care. I thought that this woman was really misinformed. CNS has been around since the 1970s. I proceeded to tell her that CNS had on-site nurses 24/7 and provided constant supervision. I explained that the only difference between CNS and a nursing home was that CNS provided a comprehensive in-patient therapy program to help someone recovering from traumatic brain injuries.

The bureaucratic tangle continued. The case manager seemed stuck on the fact that CNS was licensed as an assisted-living facility. I explained that Highmark BCBS would be paying no more for CNS than it would for a nursing home and that as a bonus Sara would get intensive therapy. I could see I was getting nowhere with this insurance bureaucrat. In response Joan and I both started writing emails to my Sunday-school class members and to our prayer chains to help resolve the situation.

Out of the blue Highmark BCBS suddenly suggested that Sara go to the other traumatic-brain-injury-treatment center in the Dallas area. The best I could figure out, the company had a deal working with a nursing home to serve as a front from an insurance perspective. While this was movement in the right direction in the red-tape department, I remained fully convinced that Sara needed to be at CNS. I adamantly stated my position.

Dave Nelson, the CEO of the software company where I worked at the time, regularly asked me how things were going with Sara. I explained to him that I was running into problems. He immediately pulled in the CFO, Phil Compton, to help. Phil reached out to the Highmark BCBS account representative, Denise Ficare. I'll always believe Denise was an angel in disguise. She spoke on the telephone with me. Then we started trading e-mails. I explained the program at CNS and how it could benefit Sara. I also told her that unlike a nursing home, CNS would be cheaper over time for the insurance company because its goal would be to make her independent, which minimizes the cost. Denise even told me, "If that were my relative (who had a brain injury), I would want them (to be) there, too."

Denise got in touch with Steve Robinson at CNS. Steve presented a strong case for Sara going to CNS. Denise had this reviewed by the company's medical director. My hopes soared. Then just as quickly my optimism was shattered. Shortly thereafter we had a response that Sara was not authorized for CNS. This was devastating, especially because time was running out for a decision to be made. The date was July 15; Sara's discharge from Baylor Rehabilitation was scheduled for July 27.

That key bureaucratic problem remained—CNS being under the assisted-living facility classification. I decided I would fight government red tape using the government's bureaucracy. I decided to reach out to the Texas Department of Insurance via my legislator. I contacted Texas State Rep. Elvira Reyna to enlist her help. Her office put me in touch with Marilyn Devine, Valerie Brown, and Sylvia Myler—all on the staff of the Texas Department of Insurance. They took my complaint and started contacting Highmark BCBS. In addition, they contacted BCBS of Texas to enlist that company's help on my behalf. If someone ever tells you that your state government doesn't go to bat for you, let him or her know my story!

In the meantime, the executives at the company at which I worked were frustrated with the lack of progress in getting Sara covered. Simultaneously the Texas Department of Insurance and my company's executive team were putting pressure on Highmark BCBS to change its ruling.

Next I decided to make a personal appeal to the Highmark BCBS CEO by writing a letter to him about my situation. Thanks to all the pressure points, Denise was able to get the medical director to reconsider his decision. Steve Robinson, Joan, and I were ecstatic! I really thought based on the momentum that this was going work.

Then it happened again! With just a few days left before discharge, the medical director ruled against Sara being admitted to CNS. This decision was quite a blow to all of us. Steve Robinson indicated he thought we had lost.

That night Joan and I prayed about the matter. She then told me, "Tim, you may have to have Welton and me living with you for the rest of our lives, but we will sell everything we have to make sure that Sara gets treatment at CNS. Tell Steve we will cover Sara at CNS and to pick her up on July 27."

Not only were Sara's parents available full time to help us — sacrificing their personal lives and willing to leave their beloved Virginia where their two sons lived, now they were willing to sacrifice financially for Sara's recovery. My parents were also ready to do what was necessary.

The next morning I called Steve Robinson to tell him to pick up Sara on Wednesday and that we would privately pay if necessary.

Meanwhile, in an attempt to be helpful, Baylor Rehabilitation suggested that Sara move to a nursing home while we got all of this straightened out. Joan and I knew that once in the nursing home, the insurance company would be extremely reluctant to even consider CNS as an alternative. In addition, psychologically Sara was prepared and excited about going to CNS. Not going there would have been a major blow to her hopes and aspirations to recover. In my mind, I could see her spiraling into depression and hopelessness if she were in a nursing home. Therefore, I simply said, "No way."

Reading the *Dallas Morning News* one day Joan spotted an article that she then left for me to read. It was about an employee of the Dallas Medical Examiner's office. He was working at his desk and suffered an acute stroke. He slumped over; passersby thought he was just taking a catnap. He died right there because he did not get the help he needed in time. I thought back to when Sara had the stroke. She was at a Parks Board meeting, which was across the street from the fire station that had the ambulance that took her to Baylor University Hospital's Emergency Room. If Sara had been at home, she probably would have been upstairs on the computer while the kids watched television downstairs. Worse yet, what if she had the stroke while driving the kids? The thought had never entered my mind before. Now I could see how I could have lost all of them! I knew that by God's grace this terrible thing that had happened to Sara had occurred in such a way that she got help and not one of the children was hurt in the process. God put her in the best place to be when the stroke occurred. She was with adults who quickly recognized the problem and summoned immediate medical attention.

At the time I believed that God's plan had been for me to see her recover and in the process teach me patience as well as to provide me an avenue to witness to others. Dr. Porter had told me that he just didn't treat stroke victims such as Sara because they just didn't survive the stroke. The Medical Examiner employee's stroke was a reminder of this fact; Sara's amazing willpower and strides were a modern miracle to me. In concrete ways they reminded me that prayer works. I remarked to Joan how lucky we were to have Sara with us.

Meanwhile, God was at work in another remarkable way—one that I would never have dreamed. The software company at which I worked was expanding in Europe and needed someone to travel and oversee the European operations. The company had just started its Central America and Latin America expansion. I had even outlined plans for Asia/Pacific. I was excited about the opportunity to help grow a start-up network software company—but a more important calling was at hand. Given my family's situation I could not continue to travel and work internationally.

My boss, Dave Nelson, understood my dilemma and decision completely. He is one guy that I would in a heartbeat nominate for "boss of the year". Not only was he a strong Christian, he also went above and beyond the call of duty for all of his employees. He perfectly understood my need to change jobs. Dave even had offered a long-term paid sabbatical, but I did not want to burden a start-up with the financial overhead of having to carry me on the payroll. I had put my heart and sole into helping the company be a success, but the time to move on had arrived.

I interviewed for a position at Cingular Wireless and was offered a job. I had never made a career decision without consulting with Sara. Fortunately, she was at least at a point that we could discuss it. I explained to her the opportunity and asked what she thought about it. I told her that the night before, I had prayed about it. I almost cried when Sara struggled to say the word Cingular. Sara said from the bed looking at me "Cing . . . u . . . lar." Shocked, I said "What?" Sara repeated and said "Cingular. You go Cingular." I couldn't believe it. I called the folks at Cingular to tell them I would be joining their team. Dave Nelson was extremely happy for me and said "Tim, this is the right thing to do. Of course, I don't want to lose you, but family comes first."

In the background I continued to stay in constant contact with my former boss and friend, Dave Nelson, and with Phil Compton. They were frustrated because of the lack of progress and contacted the Pittsburgh Technology Council. Dave was known as a mover and shaker in Pittsburgh and was able to use his connections with various technology leaders in Pittsburgh and have them contact board members of Highmark BCBS. These individuals, unknown to me, must have been angels in disguise. They persuaded the Highmark BCBS board to hear my story and push the company to cover Sara in CNS. To their credit, both of these gentlemen knew that I was leaving their company, but that made no difference to them. They both pushed very diligently to get my wife covered in CNS. Men such as Phil Compton and Dave Nelson do not come along often in anyone's lifetime. I was just fortunate that the good Lord afforded me the opportunity to get to know them, much less work for Dave.

D-Day—Wednesday, July 27, 2004—arrived and along with it time for Sara to be discharged! Joan and I instructed CNS and Baylor Rehab-imitation that CNS would pick her up and take her as an inpatient status. Things really looked bad for CNS to be covered by my insurance. Steve Robinson was very aware of all the efforts that had been undertaken to get coverage for Sara. Some were still under way:

Texas Department of Insurance was pressuring Highmark BCBS to cover Sara

Denise Ficare continued to lobby her employer's executive chain to cover Sarah at CNS.

Dave Nelson's contacts on the Pittsburgh Technology Council were pressuring the board of Highmark BCBS to have the case reviewed.

Joan put up a deposit check to cover Sara for the first couple of weeks, so we were moving forward. Denise called me Thursday to tell me she had contacted the CEO for Highmark to ask him to grant an exception and overrule the medical director. I explained that Sara was now in CNS and that we were determined to get Sara the needed treatment even if this meant going broke. Denise told me I was doing the right thing. She said she was working to get Highmark BCBS to do the right thing, too.

In the meantime I decided to work on a fourth front of attack to get insurance coverage for Sara at CNS. I started contacting the local press. *What a great human-interest story*, I thought. Sara was a mom of three school-age children and had a son going off to Iraq in the Army to serve his country in Operation Iraqi Freedom. She was a popular local community volunteer. The soccer association alone could have generated 20,000 letters to Highmark BCBS on Sara's behalf. BCBS of Texas was running local commercials on picking their plan from their employers. I believed if I could stir up enough publicity, Highmark BCBS would be under a lot of pressure from BCBS of Texas to cover Sara. The wheels were in motion. I sent an email to Steve Blow, columnist for the *Dallas Morning News*. I believed the fact that I had taught Sunday school to his son, Cory (now an adult), when he was 11-years old might help. I composed letters and emails to media outlets and personalities such as 60 Minutes, Oprah Winfrey, the local network affiliates for ABC, NBC, and CBS, as well as every level of state and federal official I could think of to help.

On Friday, July 27, 2004, I received a phone call from Denise Ficare. She told me that the CEO of Highmark BCBS had personally intervened to overturn the medical director's decision. Highmark BCBS now covered Sara for CNS. I thought of calling the CEO at Highmark to ask what changed his mind and prompted him to intervene. Was it all the prayers? BCBS of Texas? The Texas Department of Insurance? Denise Ficare? Highmark BCBS Board Members that Dave Nelson knew on the Pittsburgh Technology Council? My personal letters and emails? The copy of my letter to Steve Blow? Or the sum of all these parts? I'll never know for sure, because I didn't call. I did know that I had won a major battle and that I would need further approvals on CNS coverage from Highmark BCBS.

To contain the damage from my multi-tiered efforts, I contacted the Texas Department of Insurance and Steve Blow to ask them to hold off doing anything further. I told them Highmark BCBS was doing the right thing now; I thanked them for their support. I would wait until later to take up the battle for changes to coverage for places such as CNS. Right now, the focus had to be on Sara.

I contacted Joan to tell her the good news. She was excited! I called Steve Robinson to let him know about the Highmark decision. He was absolutely amazed and told me that this was a first. He indicated that most people never get anywhere with this type of fight. I let him know that the power of prayer does wonders and that this was a huge opportunity for Highmark BCBS to learn about the program at CNS.

Chapter 8

In-Patient at CNS

Sara arrived at CNS' inpatient facilities on Wednesday, July 27, 2004. I immediately noted that from the outside one could not tell the facility apart from its Irving, TX, neighborhood. CNS provided a unique approach to its patients; this is why Joan and I determined it was the best place for Sara. CNS bought a complex of townhomes and completely remodeled them to comply with the Americans with Disabilities Act (ADA). Each townhome contained two bedrooms, with one patient in each bedroom. Each unit had a complete kitchen, bathroom, and laundry closet. In the center of the complex CNS placed its meeting room, staff break room, and medical, security, and facility-management offices. Its nurses are on duty 24/7. The place is very secure with strict processes and procedures for visitors to follow. The facility contains a medically licensed nursing home and much more! The atmosphere is more like a home than it is a medical facility.

CNS's objective is to prepare its patients to re-enter society. A key part of its philosophy is having a facility in which the traumatically brain-injured patient learns to do simple activities (such as dressing, cleaning, washing clothes, and preparing meals) in a home setting. Each patient is assigned a caregiver who is with the patient for the entire time except during actual therapy. This caregiver receives instruction from medical personnel and caseworkers on what the patient can or can't do. For instance, some patients are ready to start re-learning how to prepare a meal, while others can only watch as the caregiver prepares the meal. The caregiver constantly monitors and writes notes on the patient's interaction with his or her environment. In addition, if the therapists assign homework, the caregiver will work with the patient to help him or her complete the assignment. The caregiver constantly reinforces the individualized treatment program for each patient. The caregiver also offers encouragement to the patient. If the patient is able to go to the grocery store, the caregiver takes the patient on the outing, assisting as much as—or as little as—is required.

Each morning the caregiver helps the patient dress. This is sometimes a very long process, because the patient is encouraged to dress himself or herself as much as possible. Occupational therapy teaches patients the skills necessary to do such ordinary, normal things as re-learning to put on a bra. Then while dressing the patient applies what has been taught in occupational therapy.

After dressing and eating breakfast patients make their short journey to the place in which therapy is provided. CNS therapy covers the basics that patients need. These basics include:

Occupational Therapy (OT)
Speech Therapy (ST)
Physical Therapy (PT)
Mental Therapy
Educational Therapy
Optical Therapy

An acquaintance of Joan had a son about Sara's age who had a stroke about the same time that Sara did. Joan told me one day she had a difficult time discussing Sara's progress with the woman. Joan and I were both excited about the progress that Sara had made and wanted to tell the world.

Regrettably when the son of Joan's friend completed his initial rehabilitation, he was referred to a nursing home, where he eventually died. Joan didn't believe she could in good conscience tell the woman about Sara's progress.

Until recently I was not aware that the best results occur when the patient receives rehabilitation immediately. The longer rehabilitation is put off, the less the recovery that occurs. The ability to recover ceases after a certain point. Medical research does not agree on the exact point at which this occurs, but six months seems to be the ballpark, critical moment at which individuals plateau. However, some believe when the family provides sufficient home assistance, some progress may be possible even years later.

Sara was excited to be at CNS. She particularly seemed to like the home setting. Sara had her own room with Internet connection. Excited by the thought of her using the Internet, I immediately moved one of our home computers to her room for her to use. I set up that computer for a left-handed person and used the disability setting for the keys.

Much to my dismay, Sara could not use the computer yet. She had much difficulty navigating the screens and knowing where to go. This was a rude awakening for me about where she was in the recovery process. Although Sara before the stroke had been proficient in Outlook, Word, Internet Explorer, and other applications on the computer, I now realized she would have to relearn all of it. As I struggled with my disappointment over this realization, I drew comfort from remembering that this also was the woman who had relearned to swallow, to talk, and to control personal functions. Sara had traveled a long distance in her recovery, but despite my hopes and dreams for her to move faster, the speed I wanted just wasn't going to happen.

At the same time, others in the rehabilitation profession

told me that Sara was making great progress. This situation drove me to my knees once again. I went home and that night prayed, "Lord Jesus, Help me to be patient. I am not patient. I know I am not, but I need to be for the kids and especially for Sara. In Jesus name I pray, Amen."

I spoke with Sara's assigned CNS case manager, Wayne Smith. Wayne took over from Steve Robinson. Steve had done a wonderful job dotting the i's and crossing the t's to get Sara into CNS. Now Wayne's job was to provide oversight for Sara's care inside CNS. He gathered information from the therapy groups about Sara's case and monitored the situation to be sure she was making progress. He explained that CNS personnel operated as a team and provided a holistic approach to Sara's care. Sara's team would pore over the notes from the caregivers and provide additional instructions. I was impressed with how well this system sounded, so once again I had high hopes for Sara's progress.

I watched the therapists and Wayne interact with Sara and the other patients. I could not imagine the job satisfaction these individuals receive in dealing with patients. I decided that being a therapist and having an impact on someone's life must be the most satisfying job in the world.

Within two weeks CNS had completed its formal assessment of Sara. CNS has a grading scale with a range from 1 to 100 (100 being able to live independently). CNS rated Sara at 26. When Wayne provided Joan and me the score, we were disappointed. Her low score reinforced how far Sara had to go. Being a very impatient person, I wanted her back at 100 percent immediately. Once again I was reminded that things just weren't going to happen my way.

Joan and I worked out a schedule to insure that one of us visited Sara each evening. In addition, we worked on the schedule to insure the kids visited Sara on a regular basis. I knew in my heart that the kids needed to be there to see their mother's slow progress and to reassure them that someday she would return home. I also believed that Sara's having constant contact with the kids was important. I wanted to reinforce the fact that she is their mom and that they needed her. The kids and I had a great time going to visit Sara. Since the caregiver did not provide meals for the family, I would pick up a take-out order at a local restaurant for all of us, including Sara. The kids were having a great time and often told me that they could see the progress in Sara. This gave them hope.

I also was very concerned about the kids' well being. I knew the shock of instantly not having their mother at home and her being in the hospital for an extended period would make a huge impact on them emotionally. Fortunately, Joan had much experience in this area. For years she had been a kindergarten teacher. We had several discussions about the kids. I told her that I wanted the kids to have a normal life while we worked through this situation. I said I was worried about them.

Joan gave me some sobering advice. She told me that in her experience kids are somewhat selfish. She said they first want to know how a circumstance is going to affect them. Once they realize their lives will not be changed dramatically, then they are free to process the issues facing their sick parent. From day one of the stroke, my dad, my niece, Joan and others worked diligently to keep the kids on their regular schedule of activities including soccer and school. Joan and I saw the kids' comments and questions about their mother's recovery as good signs they were hoping she would return home soon. We agreed the kids' day-to-day lives were not affected by their mother's illness and disability.

Shortly after Sara moved to CNS, I received my official offer from Cingular. My start date was August 23, 2004. Since

I had never had to deal with insurance issues when considering employment, I presumed everything in the transition would go well. I had been assured that I could sign up with Blue Cross-Blue Shield of Texas and after 30 days would have no problem with pre-existing conditions. I was on top of the world or at least as much as I could be given the circumstances. I believed in my heart that my wife was in a place that would help her recover, the insurance would cover everything, and I was going to have a job in which I could be with my family more often. My mother-in-law was there and now talking about Welton retiring and moving in to help with the kids. What I didn't realize was that God had other plans for me!

Chapter 9

Battle Number 2

My soon-to-be ex-boss, Dave Nelson, was extremely supportive of my move to Cingular. He even told me that he would cover my medical insurance until Cingular's insurance kicked in. This was very reassuring and generous. I at first told Dave he didn't have to do this, but he insisted saying, "You have done a lot for this company. It is my way of thanking you." Knowing Dave, I suspect he would do that for any employee. As I've said before, he was an outstanding boss. Few people in my career have impressed me as Dave did with their ethical standards and Christian values.

Things for Sara were going well at CNS. The caregivers and the administrator at the in-patient facility told me how much they liked working with Sara. I was told that she had a positive attitude and the staff was impressed with her family's support. In fact the administrator told me that the caregivers actually fought over who would get to care for Sara. Sara's willpower and determination impressed everyone including me. Sara did not want anyone doing anything for her that she could do herself. Her language skills were improving; she could communicate much better. "No! I do it," she would say when she wanted to do something and didn't want any help.

CNS held monthly meetings with Joan and me to discuss Sara's progress. These were quite extensive and included reports from each of the five areas of therapy—occupational, speech, physical, mental, and educational. I would walk away from these meetings with a 50 or more page document outlining Sara's progress against current goals and listing any new goals for her. In one of these meetings Wayne and I discussed Sara's positive attitude. Because of it Sara had made a lot of progress, he said. Wayne again attributed part of Sara's progress to her family support. I told him that I had prayed that she would stay focused and have a positive attitude. He then told me something disturbing about patients going through rehabilitation. Wayne said many patients have a lot of issues and are depressed. In addition, he explained that some patients do not have a supportive family. He said many families get upset with the situation and believe the individual going through rehabilitation is a burden. Some even blame the individual for having the stroke and exhibit anger toward them." Wayne said sometimes the patients are older and their caregivers are their adult children. Sometimes the patient is younger and the angry spouse is the caregiver, he said. He said this was why CNS offers counseling to spouses and other family members.

This revelation really troubled me. I wondered why marriage vows were taken so lightly. I could understand why children get angry but not spouses and adult children. I decided that having a Christian-based relationship and household does make a difference. I'm not saying that a Christian foundation prevents one from getting angry. We are all human.

These revelations sparked within me a desire to deliver the following message to families of stroke victims:

1. No matter how you feel, insure that you maintain a positive attitude with your loved one with a stroke.

2. Visit the person often and provide encouragement.

3. Even if you are not a member of a local church, reach out to a church for help. You will be surprised how much local churches want to help.

4. Remember, going through stroke recovery is not something you have to face alone.

I started work with Cingular. Immediately because of the AT&T Wireless acquisition, which was under way, I had a heavy workload. My job started to consume a large part of my time, because I had to spend a considerable amount of time at Cingular's headquarters in Atlanta.

With every trip that I made, I realized more and more how much I appreciated Joan's help. Where else could I find someone who would care and love my kids like this grandmother did and would sacrifice in order to do so? I learned that Joan had a history of doing this. When Joan was a young adult, her mother died of cancer. She and Welton took in Joan's younger sister to rear.

At Cingular, I debated which insurance carrier I should sign up with and even discussed the matter with CNS. I chose Blue Cross Blue Shield and did not realize the company was BCBS of Georgia, not Texas. I don't know how I missed this significant point. I guess I was just fat, dumb, and overly optimistic. I naively presumed I was in great shape!

As I was making the choice about insurance carriers, the Terry Schiavo case was in the news big time. This became a topic of conversation everywhere, including in our home. At first I was appalled to read that Terry's husband had moved in with another woman and had a child by her. "I would never do this with Sara," I said. It was easy for me to take this high moral ground. Still, the Schiavo case weighed heavily on my heart. I could empathize with Terry's husband. I had a wife whom the doctor's projected " . . . would not walk, talk, or interact with anyone." I do not know all the medical facts of the Schiavo case, but our projected outcome was very similar to the Schiavos' situation.

As I reflected and discussed it with Joan, I began to see huge differences between the situations involving Terry's husband and myself. Terry and her husband were married a short-time when she suffered the brain damage. They had no children. Sara and I had been married 19 years. Together we had three children; I had reared Sara's son since he was 3.

I thought, *Sara and I have been married a long time. Of course, when you first get married, a large percentage of the relationship is physical attraction. I am not saying I didn't love Sara, but love matures over time. After many years together you love the person and value the relationship over any physical attraction. Terry's husband never had the opportunity that I had to mature in his love for Terry. Like me and many other men, he probably wanted children. I can't say that if I had been his age at the time of the stroke I wouldn't have done the same that he did. He never had the opportunity for maturity to happen naturally. A physical relationship is not something that is long lasting. At this stage in life, if Sara and I never have sex again, I would always be faithful and support her, because my love is on a different plane.*

My knee-jerk reaction was disgust toward Terry's husband. I thought he should turn her over to her parents. Yet I realized I might have done the same thing he did if I were not a Christian and were still a young man. I also understood fully that God says we are not to judge others. Too many of my fellow Christians were into judging Mr. Schiavo. That really bothered me. All I knew about myself was that I wanted to stay by Sara's side. I did not want to give up on her.

As I sat getting ready for bed the evening Terry Schiavo died, I got out my Bible, read it, and reflected back on my thoughts about my love being on a different plane. I thought, *Wow. I can see parallels here to our relationship with God! When Pharaoh let the Israelites go, we had a God who did a lot for His people. He protected them; He insured that they had food; He guided them to the Promised Land. All through these times, God established a very physical relationship with humankind. While God didn't change, we humans matured in our relationship with God. God gave His only son, Jesus, who died for our sins so that we might enter the gates of Heaven. This is a very physical relationship. Over time, we humans have matured in our relationship with God. After Jesus rose again, the early church was formed and humankind's worship changed. Even a new Christian has a physical relationship focus. A new Christian goes to church to do the Christian things. As her or she matures, he or she may still do these "Christian" things, but their relationship with God has gone way beyond the physical. They have what I would call a mental and emotional relationship with God.*

In my thoughts I hope I haven't committed heresy here, but this was a revelation that helped me understand some deeper issues the Schiavo case raised in my mind. Certainly my maturity as a Christian has helped me with self-reflection and made me less judgmental.

The trip to Irving from Mesquite became routine for the kids, Joan and me. Joan, the super organizer, had all of the kid's schedules written down. This included when each child was to visit Sara. We didn't take all three kids at one time to see Sara because that would have been just too much for Sara (and her roommate) to manage, plus it gave each child one-on-one time with Sara.

Joshua, who no longer was living at home, made regular trips to see his mother. We had not told Sara about Joshua's upcoming deployment to Iraq. The time was drawing near for him to go, so I gave Joshua permission to tell Sara. Joshua was activated as part of the 56th BCT (Brigade Combat Team) from the Texas National Guard. He was headed to Fort Hood for training to prepare him to support Operation Iraqi Freedom. Joshua told Sara, "Mom. I volunteered to go. I know a lot of older guys and guys with families who could be going instead of me. If I go, then that means that some guy with a family doesn't have to go. I also feel that I have a duty to my country to support the war in Iraq."

Sara took this news very well. She indicated she was proud of him. Of course, she worried about Joshua and told me so. She also saw that he was maturing and growing into a man anyone would be pleased to have as a son. He told me that he probably could have gotten out of his tour of duty because of his mother's illness, but he believed he should not do that but should go. I supported him on this decision.

I could write three or four books and never do justice to the determination and willpower that I witnessed in Sara. She made daily progress and I knew it, but that progress wasn't always as apparent to an impatient person like me. I knew something positive was happening when a person who hadn't seen her for two or three weeks visited. They were always shocked at her progress. I kept thinking to myself, *Yeah, she has made progress, but not like you are expressing.* She was, however, making progress. I just didn't see it as clearly because I saw her so often. The best analogy that I can share with you is that of your kids. Anyone who has reared children has experience the following statement, "Wow, your kids have grown so much!" You don't see that your kids have grown, because you see them every day. Their growth, however, is a shock to others. Of course, the time you realize your kids are growing is when you have to buy new clothes because they have outgrown their old ones. This was my barometer on my kids' growth.

By October 1, my new insurance through Cingular Wireless had kicked in. I had subsequently found out that BCBS of Georgia was handling the case. I asked the new insurance carrier to get in contact with Wayne Smith and Steve Robinson at CNS. We were hopeful that the transition would be uneventful. Besides, we had precedence with both BCBS of Texas and Highmark BCBS of Pennsylvania supporting Sara being at CNS. The BCBS of Georgia case manager called to introduce herself and indicated that she had worked with Wayne to get Sara covered at CNS. Everything was going well, or so I thought. The case manager seemed nice enough. She had managed to get CNS covered by working through BCBS of Texas. Plus, Cingular's coverage was self-funded. That meant Cingular only paid BCBS of Georgia to administrate its program.

I received a call from the caseworker saying Sara's stay at CNS had been authorized and everything was on track. That same day I decided to follow-up on my Social Security filing. *This painful experience of spending 12 hours filling out paperwork and waiting in lines should be worth it*, I reasoned. I would need the money to help with Sara. I also thought, *I've paid more to Social Security in 10 years than most people pay in their lifetimes.* I believed the program would be there to support us when we needed it. Despite the negative publicity I supported the program and only hoped that then-President Bush's plan to salvage it worked. A Social Security official said she they would get back with me, so I patiently waited again. I knew it would take a few months based on Joan's feedback about how long it took her brother Jerry to get disability. Meanwhile I called Wayne to discuss Sara's case. He told me something that seemed disturbing about BCBS of Georgia. Wayne started telling me how difficult it was to work with the new case manager at BCBS of Georgia. He indicated that she had put him through a big hassle just to get Sara authorized and that she was only authorized for two weeks at a time. Wayne indicated that in 20 years, this was the worst experience that he had with a case manager. Since the case manager had told me that everything was going great and put a real positive spin on everything, this conversation set off alarm bells in my head. I decided to document everything the case manager said and compare my notes with those of Wayne.

I am no expert on the modern health care and insurance system. However, I have found some things out through the School of Hard Knocks. If you are not aware of how the system works, understand one thing: The case manager assigned to you is your portal into your insurance provider. The way that the person "spins" the situation and document it has a lot to do with your quality of coverage. Hopefully, you never irritate the person with whom you have to work. Since I had a bad experience with the case manager at Highmark BCBS of Pennsylvania, I decided to start validating her knowledge of traumatic brain injuries and strokes. This new case manager did not have a clue about the topic. In fact, my mother-in-law and I both had conversations with her about the program at CNS and how it was benefiting Sara. In each conversation, documented by me, the case manager was not aware of the treatment program at CNS. This was odd because weekly she was getting 20- to 50-page reports. She had not read the document provided to her. All I knew was this was not going good.

The case manager fills a dual role with conflicting interests. First, the person is the patient's representative. The person is supposed to be an advocate for the patient's rights under the insurance coverage. On the other hand, the person is supposed to be the watchdog to prevent abuse of the insurance coverage and works to minimize the cash outlay to their employer. I know that it is a difficult role but one that needs to be carried out with professional and ethical civility.

In the middle of this upset with the insurance provider, I received a letter from the Social Security administration. It included a letter stating, "Your benefits have been processed and your coverage is attached." However, nothing was in the letter or anything explaining coverage or what Sara was entitled to. *Strange*, I thought. I called and could not get a good answer. I made the trip to the local office and waited in line several hours. I finally got to talk to a clerk. She told me, "Sara is eligible for Medicare in about two years, but she has no coverage for disability." Shocked, I said, "What do you mean no coverage? She worked and I have worked. Why isn't she covered?" This was when I discovered a huge flaw in our Social Security system. The clerk replied, "Sara has worked for the community college system in Dallas County. They do not participate in Social Security. Therefore, she has not paid anything into Social Security in the past 10 years. We use that as our means of determining whether someone is eligible for Social Security. Sara has no coverage. You will need to go to the Dallas County Community College to get her disability coverage."

At this point I became furious. I still get angry when I think about it, but as a Christian I try to temper my anger. I wasn't sure whether I was mad that I spent 12 hours filling out the paperwork and waiting in lines, mad at myself for not knowing that Sara wasn't paying Social Security, or mad that Sara and the kids were not going to get some type of help from the Social Security Administration because of Sara's disability. Besides, I had paid the maximum tax for several years. I thought about the stay-at-home moms (and stay-at-home dads these days) who rear their kids and keep an environment that allows their spouse to work. I asked the clerk about the fact that Sara was really a stay-at-home mom. She told me that if someone doesn't work at a job and doesn't pay into Social Security, the person is not eligible for disability benefits. The clerk reported that if someone works part-time and pays Social Security taxes, the person would be eligible for disability based on the amount of credits paid. This was the first time I realized that our system penalizes stay-at-home parents and doesn't provide them with disability coverage. I believe firmly if one spouse is working full time and the other is staying with the kids, then Social Security should do something to provide disability benefits. I thought for a moment that I ought to run for Congress and get this gap fixed, but once again I reminded myself that my focus needed to be on Sara. I did take the time out to educate my church on this problem. I also sent a note to Sara's fellow workers. The county community college system was mostly made up of part-time employees who do not get benefits. Many were shocked to find out that they had no Social Security coverage. One solution might be for the working spouse to pay the nonworking spouse a small salary or wage so Social Security taxes could be paid and benefits accrued. I did find out that if I died, Sara and the kids would get benefits.

Things seemed bad, but I quickly reasoned that they were not that bad. I computed that if I kept working at my same level, Sara and I still would be able to retired at a reasonable age. I did realize I would have to do more retirement planning.

While contemplating Social Security's shortcomings, I received a call from Wayne Smith at CNS. Wayne said, "Tim, BCBS of Georgia is planning on Sara being discharged by the 15th."

I could not believe what I was hearing. Discharged? CNS was making the case of medical necessity for her to be there at least until November. Despite the doctor's recommendation BCBS of Georgia was pushing for her to be discharged immediately. I thanked Wayne for the heads-up and told him to keep fighting with the insurance company. My next call was to the caseworker. She explained that the medical director had denied the claim. I told her that this was unbelievable. I asked if she had communicated the recommendation from Sara's doctor about medical necessity. I asked her if she was aware of the recommendation in the last report. She did not know about the last report. I asked her other details the report provided about Sara. The caseworker did not have a clue and obviously had not been reading the reports on Sara. I called Wayne back. He told me that she refused to discuss the situation with him. He said she told him that I had agreed to the discharge. Something was dramatically wrong here. I drew the conclusion the case-worker was trying to derail my wife's case to stay in CNS.

Suddenly I was in a desperate mode. I decided to reach out to the CEO of BCBS of Georgia. I believed I had documented proof that the case manager was not doing her job correctly. I actually believed I had evidence of several inaccuracies between what she was telling Wayne at CNS and what she was telling me. Fortunately, Wayne and I were in constant communication. As soon as the caseworker called either of us, we would call the other. Wayne was as committed as I was to insuring Sara got the care she needed. While I was spending time tracking down the contact information for the CEO of BCBS of Georgia, I sent a letter to the company and requested a new case manager. Right after that I composed my e-mail to the CEO of BCBS of Georgia. I explained that we both had wives about the same age and children in the same age range. I appealed to him about what he would want for his wife and stated clearly my belief that the case manager was not repre-senting my wife's best interests. The CEO sent me a personal email indicating that he would look into my situation.

The next day, I received a letter from the medical director

at BCBS of Georgia denying my appeal of his judgment and also telling me that my request to have a new case manager was denied. I called his office and was told he didn't have time to talk with me. My conversation with the caseworker turned very hostile. She told me to prepare to have my wife at home. I explained to her that she had admitted not even reading the 20- to 50-page report that she asked CNS to generate. I was told that the report didn't matter and that Sara was going home. Then, as if the situation was not confusing enough, the medical director's office called and said that they would extend Sara another week or so for us to prepare having Sara at home.

The good news in all this was that CNS had helped Sara progress to the point in which we didn't need to acquire a stair lift to help her to the second floor. This was an amazing advance that probably got lost at this point because I was engaged in a battle with BCBS of Georgia. In particular, the medical director and case manager were at odds with me. I was not going to lose. I had prayed and firmly believe that God was behind me. If you have no faith, I feel sorry that you may never experience the power that you can feel when you have God on your side. I can't explain it, but I felt that way at that point in my life. Bravado was not operational here; faith and belief in Jesus gave me power at that point in my life. I would hope that everyone would have this opportunity because it is not an exclusive club. All you have to do is have faith in Jesus Christ and accept Him as your Lord and Savior.

We made preparations to move Sara home as BCBS of Georgia was preparing to cut off Sara's coverage in rehabilitation based on the case manager's input and the recommendation of the medical director. CNS sent the occupational therapist to our home to evaluate the settings and determine what changes were needed. Again, to my amazement, Sara did not need a stair lift! Just two months before I had been looking at home elevators and stair lifts. A miracle was happening before my eyes. In addition, my parents and in-laws were setting incredible examples for my children. My dad, who is retired, showed up at our house and widened the door to the bathroom and basically made our master bathroom ADA compliant. This was no easy task and involved moving electrical switches and a lot of diligent work. My dad did this to help and never charged me a penny! This type of family support should be the model for the modern Christian family. Government and aide agencies can't provide the emotional support that a family can give in a time of crisis or when someone is facing challenges. I am extremely lucky to have such great parents and in-laws. I also had something else helping me face the situation. I had a relationship with God and a wonderful church family. I had a mission to make sure that Sara knew that she had support and that she didn't feel alone. I also know that I now had personal experience and could empathize and provide witness to those in need. If anyone reading this doesn't have a church home and is facing something like I have in my life, I encourage you to reach out for help. Your local church can be your family.

I wrote a personal appeal to the CEO of BCBS of Georgia. I explained the notes that I had taken about the discrepancies of the case manager's stories to both Wayne and me. I told him I believe she had not read the reports that CNS had generated for her. I also cited my firm belief that the case manager was hostile toward me. Since BCBS of Georgia had indicated Sara would not be covered as an inpatient, I went ahead and person-ally covered the costs for her to stay at CNS through the end of October. I figured it was a goodwill gesture on my part and was hoping that BCBS of Georgia would cover Sara's outpa-tient visits. Sara would be coming home in the next few days; we were getting ready for her. I had fought the good fight.

I hoped the medical director and case manager would recognize the necessity of Sara's continued rehabilitation at CNS. Instead, Sara appeared to be just another liability to them. In all candor and honesty, I'm sure the case manager, for the rest of her career, will cite me as a problem to her. She probably thinks as poorly of me as I do of her. I had challenged her from day one and was not about to back down or accept what I believed to be sub-par customer service from her. I also had another point. I firmly believed that God was behind me. I know that this may sound absurd to some, but my dreams, my prayers, and what had been revealed to me firmly made me believe that I would win. In this day and time people just don't open up and have faith. We have computers, electronic services, and science. Who needs God? We control our own destiny. I had been guilty of feeling this way. When I did, I was wrong! When you feel like this, God has a way of reminding you Who is in control. I had been reminded of Who is in control. I knew this and also knew that God was on Sara's side.

Shortly after Sara moved home—a joyful experience, I will say—I received a call from BCBS of Georgia. Sara was adapting well, but I was really concerned about outpatient coverage. The call that I received was from a woman who said she was the director of customer relations for BCBS of Georgia. She then explained that seven other people were on the conference call including the medical director, director of case management, and director of major accounts. I thought that I must have been hearing an angel's voice. She then went on to explain that I had a new case manager named Faye Redding. If Sara had been nearby, I would have said to pinch me to make sure that I was awake. The director of customer relations indicated that the CEO had asked her personally to intervene and manage Sara's case. She personally committed that Sara's outpatient coverage would be extended through the next few months. She told me there would be no more one- to two-week extensions. She also told me that Faye was one of their specialists in complex cases and would be working Sara's case. I thought "Wow!" I was about to exclaim *Hallelujah!* Faye indicated that she would call me, so I thanked everyone on the call for his or her support. Clearly the CEO of BCBS of Georgia was going to become another of my heroes alongside Denise Ficare of Highmark BCBS of Pennsylvania.

Chapter 10

Returning Home

While Joan and I believed that Sara could use another month as a patient at CNS, we were both excited for her to be moving home. I had paid out of our personal funds her additional time as a CNS patient after BCBS of Georgia stopped its in-patient coverage. Though short, the time was sufficient to mitigate the risks to Sara. BCBS of Georgia should have covered this cost and probably an additional month. However, at least it now would cover the outpatient portion.

Jeremy, Tiffany, and Tricia were excited that Sara would be moving home. I don't think I ever realized the full emotional impact Sara's illness had on them, though I did spend a lot of time in prayer asking God to help our children with the situation. Joshua, who was at Fort Hood preparing for deployment to Iraq, was excited too. The Army kept him very busy, but he managed to call on a weekly basis. Seeing firsthand their mother improving on a constant basis helped the kids still at home. Seeing the kids regularly kept Sara motivated about returning home. I just could not have imagined her being in a nursing home. We were all so glad the kids had not lost their mother and I had not lost my wife. She was going to be an active part of our lives again and be the mother the children so desperately needed.

As previously mentioned, CNS has family conferences once a month. Sara was slated to return home on November 1. We had a conference with CNS staff just before Sara's return home. As usual Sara's progress continued to amaze me. In addition Wayne presented me with great news. Earlier, within the first two weeks of Sara's being admitted as an in-patient at their facility, CNS had completed a formal assessment of Sara. In that evaluation Sara had been rated at 26. Instead, Wayne said that Sara had progressed to a 76. I had been disappointed at the 26 number but was elated at the 76. This told me that the program was working. This was evident within Sara herself. My interactions with her at CNS were becoming more like conversations. I knew she had a ways to go, but my wife was recovering and was returning home!

A week or so prior to Sara's return home, I read an article in the *Dallas Morning News* about a 45-year-old Baptist pastor from South Korea. The pastor had suffered an acute stroke just as Sara had. Don't you find funny the fact that you start noticing things that happen to others after something happens to you personally? My wife had a stroke. For this reason I now started to notice articles about strokes, meet people who had had strokes, etc. This article really got to me. About two years earlier the Korean pastor had suffered a stroke. His wife took care of him at home. All he could do was wiggle one finger. When you are feeling a little down, all you have to do is look around you and realize how blessed you are. Everything is a matter of perspective. I kept the pastor in my prayers, as I do for all stroke victims that I encounter or learn about.

When Sara first arrived home, life was challenging. Although she could walk up the stairs, she was really tired when she did so. Joan made the recommendation that Sara only go upstairs at bedtime. Sara still needed monitoring when she needed to go to the bathroom. During the first month home she seemed to need to go every three or four hours. This interrupted my sleep in the middle of the night. Sara apologized to me when she needed to get up. This was really tough on me, because I knew that she wanted to be the one taking care of me. Sara told me she didn't want to be a burden. It was no bother to me. I knew if I showed any signs of strain from getting up, she would misinterpret it. Mothers reading this book will probably better understand what I about to say. The fathers may if they paid attention and watched their wives with their children. This is the only analogy I can think of to describe my feelings at the time. A mother naturally takes care of her child. She doesn't see it as a chore or burden. It is not an obligation but something mothers do out of love. That was the same way I felt about helping and taking care of Sara. Some people refer to it as a *labor of love*. I was so happy that I could help her. I often thought of not being able to help her. What if she were in a nursing home? I was so happy for her to be home.

Sara broke down a couple of times and cried. She told me she didn't want to be a burden. Her tears made me want to cry, too. In order to keep from crying, truthfully I had to bite my tongue and lip so solidly they bled. I was taught that little boys don't cry. Maybe that's wrong by today's standards, but that was how I was reared.

Over time Sara accepted my help more readily. At the same time, I saw her becoming more and more independent. I say again: I have never seen anyone with so much drive, grit, and determination. If our kids have even a fraction of what Sara has, I will never have to worry about them. When Sara was an in-patient at CNS, she had the assistance of the caregiver. When she got home, Sara was facing her husband or her mother helping her with everything from fixing her hair to helping clip her bra. I never knew how much we use both hands on even the most minimal tasks. Sara struggled and kept trying. She also didn't want my help! Finally, when time was pressing against being on time for going somewhere, she would relent and let me help. I want to go on record about bras! I have never worn one except when I was 6 and took my Army helmet and pretend rifle into the living room to embarrass my teen-age sister with her visiting boyfriend. Even though that was a long time ago, I will never forget how embarrassed she was. Her boyfriend was cool about it and didn't say anything. That didn't matter, because I was dead meat. It probably took her years to get over it. Well, back to the bras . . .. Bras are something that teen-age boys dream about taking off. I can still remember my friends bragging about being able to snap off a girl's bra. I never had the opportunity to practice and really attributed most of the stories to male bravado. After I helped Sara with her bra, I am now firmly convinced that all of the boys that told me this were boasting about desire, not fact. I had trouble taking the bra off. Worse, bras are a pain to put on. What moron would invent something that has the hooks in the back and expect someone to reach around and attach the two ends of the bra together? The little hooks have to go in small minute little catches that you can't even see! A bra that snaps in the front is a much better idea.

Shaving a woman's legs was another interesting lesson for me. This was another area in which I had no experience whatsoever. I remember that for a commercial former quarterback Joe Namath shaved his legs. I thought that was funny. Sara was embarrassed for me to help her shave her legs, but I told her I enjoyed doing such things for her.

Today, Sara can completely dress herself and does everything without a need for my help. To understand the effort that someone with one arm goes through, try dressing with one arm. I tried and fell in the closet three times; I didn't have the complications of something like a bra!

Sara continued to have difficulty finding the right words to use in conversations. I tried to be very patient and would wait for her to find the words. About 75 percent of the time, if I waited, she could find the correct words. If she couldn't find the words, either I or someone else would help her. In addition to the great speech therapy program at CNS our family helped Sara with this issue by asking her to repeat a sentence after we have helped her find the right words to use. For instance, one time Sara wanted to ask for the lotion but could not find the right words. She could, however, point. (A person with aphasia—brain damage to the speech center, which affects the ability to speak—can communicate non-verbally.) From her pointing I knew what Sara wanted. Instead of merely handing her the lotion, I said *lotion* and asked her to repeat it. She said *lotion*. Then I asked her to repeat, "Please hand me the lotion." Sara repeated the sentence; I handed her the lotion. In effect, Sara was rebuilding her ability to speak. The brain is amazing and often finds a way to make those neural connections.

I cannot understate the role the family plays in helping a stroke victim regain such abilities as speech. The easiest approach would be to just hand her the lotion. The best approach is to use each incident such as this as a learning experience.

Slowly, over weeks, Sara would start asking for things or making normal conversation comments about things discussed previously. As I've said many times already, I am a very impatient person. I am also a typical male. I just want to fix things and move on. I had to learn that practicing patience and doing the right thing—not the expedient thing—was best long-term for both Sara and our family. I firmly believe patience is the key for the spouse or family member. I am not a rehabilitation expert, but I do know that we were consistent in our approach to speech and still follow this practice even today. Occasionally Sara still finds a word she can't say, but this happens less often.

Another area that we had to address with the kids was

completing Sara's sentences for her. Sara was slow in her speech, but the kids were quick to pick up on what she was trying to say. They would jump right in and complete the sentences for her. Sara didn't really mind this, because she got her message out. However, we wanted Sara to practice.

This is a difficult message to get across to a 7- and a 10-year old. Joan did an excellent job explaining the situation to the kids. A mandatory training class I took at Cingular reinforced this practice. The class was about dealing with individuals who have disabilities. In the part covering speech impediments, the instructions were very clear and very appropriate for Sara: be patient, do not complete sentences, and even offer other forms of communication (e.g. writing). Since we wanted Sara to practice, we did not give her the choice to use those other forms of communciation.

In the 1950s the black-and-white TV show "Father Knows Best" depicted ideal family life of that era. Many of the ideals in that show are difficult to implement today with longer commutes and many more complications from modern society. But those ideals still linger in our minds and thoughts. One of those ideal images was the way the family in "Father Knows Best" ate dinner together every night. The father worked a 9-to-5 job and his office was near the home, so the family ate at exactly 5:30 each evening. In our family, this is pure fiction. I'm rarely ever able to get home by 6 p.m. and then only when I'm in town.

Still through Sara's illness we've learned the importance of consistency—another lesson that "Father Knows Best" modeled for us. Even when I'm not available, Sara, Joan, Welton, and the kids try to eat dinner at 6 p.m. daily. This consistency is just one more factor that seems to help Sara in her recovery.

Sara continued in her outpatient rehab program at CNS, which continued to help her. But instead of calling it therapy or rehabilitation, she looked on CNS as her "school". She says she is relearning many things that were lost in the stroke. As she changed our perspective on looking at her re-training, Joan, Welton, the kids, and I could all see how her re-framing the situation helped to keep her—and us—on track even to this day.

Chapter 11

Improvements

From the first day Sara arrived home, she continued to improve.

Periodically Sara would say, "Look at what I can do." Typically these were responses to physical actions or occupational therapy-type activities. (Remember: Occupational therapy refers to the little things that many of us take for granted. These things include such tasks as putting on a dress or opening a can of soup. It can even be those tasks associated with relearning a trade.)

After about 12 weeks Sara could dress herself completely. I had to help or monitor her doing such things as getting into the shower, getting in or out of bed, transferring from a wheelchair to the commode, and so forth. The increase in her abilities was nothing short of amazing.

Sara's ability to dress herself completely occurred so slowly over time that I barely realized what was happening. Then all of a sudden one day she didn't need my help at all to dress. I realized I wasn't getting up in the middle of the night, I wasn't helping her shave her legs, I wasn't helping with the bra, and I wasn't helping her with her hair. I was stunned when I realized I wasn't helping. So even at nine, 10, or 11 months, she experienced unnoticeable, gradual improvement about which those involved with the care of a stroke victim have to be patient.

Fixing Sara's hair presented a real challenge for me, but this, too, became her total responsibility just three months after her return home. An interesting fact was how in the beginning she and I settled for a just-get-it-done. As she improved, so did her desire for better looking hairdos. I must admit God did not design me to be a beautician, even though my mother was one for more than 30 years. Pulling a ponytail tightly will never be my favorite thing to do! Still, I was able to accomplish the task.

When Sara dressed and I helped, we focused on the basics—get the clothes on, fix the hair, and so forth. As time passed, Sara was much more conscious about her appearance and looks and not just her hairdos. In the beginning I might have to assist a little with makeup. This progressed over the months. Sara started wanting help with earrings, necklaces, and other items of jewelry. Before I know it, we were doing the whole makeup thing—the eyeliner, base, eye shadow, power and lipstick. Because even with one hand she did it better than with my two hands, she quickly became proficient at putting on her makeup. About the only time I had to assist was to track down two daughters who had developed a growing interest in makeup. The girls would borrow their mother's makeup; then I would have to go and retrieve it. That is no longer problem today, because we buy makeup for the girls as well as for Sara.

Eventually Sara began focusing on how certain clothes looked together on her. She would get out various items and then ask my opinion about whether they belonged together. I knew she was progressing very well when she started telling me what I ought to wear—or rather, what I ought not to wear together!

Sara also started to rekindle her mathematics skills. While she continued at CNS and often had homework related to everything from English to reading, she became almost obsessed at working mathematical problems. She had all of the books and materials from when she worked at Eastfield College. These books included basic elementary mathematics to advanced topics such as trigonometry and calculus. Sara started out with the basic math problems. She would ask her mom or me check them to insure that she gotten them correct. Eventually she checked her own work. Sara developed an interest in Sudoku, a mathematical puzzle found in the newspaper each day. She really enjoyed these puzzles. They have various levels; she progressed right through all the levels. I bought a Sudoku book for her; the rest is history!

Each of us performs many, many tasks each day. Often we are not aware of what all we do because some of them, such as tying our shoelaces, buttoning our clothes, and washing our hands, are so routine we hardly notice them. Because of Sara's stroke, these small, seemingly insignificant things became major markers of her progress. I firmly believe that if Sara had been confined to a nursing home, these improvements would not have occurred. Instead, we chose to not take the easy route to the nursing home but to work diligently to help Sara recover as much as possible.

Meanwhile, our new representative from BCBS of Georgia, Faye Redding, turned out to be a Godsend. Faye brought to Sara's case significant knowledgeable about strokes and traumatic brain-injury recoveries. She described her job as a "complex-case" manager. Wayne told us Faye understood everything he told her and was a pleasure to work with! I told fellow employees at Cingular how pleased I was with BCBS of Georgia.

At this point, things were going great—or so I thought.

Chapter 12

Medtronic

While Sara constantly improved, one battle she waged was between mobility and mental recovery. I know this sounds strange, but the two were often are war with one another. Sara suffered from what I would term severe spasticity; this affected her left-side extremities. Since she had no use of her right arm and hand, the impact was on her right leg. The leg would become so tense she could not bend it. Sometimes it would take all of my strength to help get her right leg to bend. Think of her situation as like having to walk around with a full-length cast on your leg. To counter this, Sara took Baclofin. This drug helped patients with this condition. However, in severe cases, taking enough of this drug causes a person to be tired or sleepy. Consequently, taking enough Baclofin to increase Sara's mobility and even work with her hand made her tired. This impacted the progress of her mental recovery. If I had to have a choice, I would prefer for Sara to recover mentally than to recover her mobility.

Dr. Rappa, the medical director at CNS, suggested Sara consider a Medtronic Baclofin pump. He said the pump could deliver the medicine directly to her spinal fluid and exponentially reduce the dosage required when it is taken orally. In turn he said this would help with Sara's spasticity and also her feeling tired. Sara vehemently opposed the idea because it involved placing inside her a battery-operated pump with a catheter to her spinal column.

This issue arose while we were all observing a major transformation in Sara. After the stroke, Joan and I made all of the decisions for Sara. Now Sara wanted to be in control of her destiny. In other words Sara had gone from being a person guided in her destiny to one who very much was in control of herself and her future.

Unlike with previous major decisions Joan and I now needed to learn more about the Medtronic pump and to work with Sara to overcome her objections. But first Joan and I had to be convinced this was the right solution to pursue.

Medtronic is one of those companies that started out of the founder's garage and has grown into a medical company with a major impact. It makes everything from defibrillators that can actually restart the heart automatically to pumps to dispense medicine. Medtronic is a success story in itself and probably worthy of a book on the impact the company has on people's lives. I researched Medtronic to understand what the company was all about since I had not heard of it. From a financial standpoint everything checked out; it was a great company doing great things.

Joan and I reviewed the material on the Baclofin pump. It showed people such as Sara with severe spasticity able to regain mobility. On one promotional video a man who had a brain injury was able to go back to woodworking in his shop. I always have reservations about anything that sounds too good to be true. Some people might use the term "doubting Thomas" to refer to people such as I am.

Now convinced ourselves, Joan and I decided we needed to persuade Sara to try the pump. We showed her the video and discussed issues such as maintenance. Once implanted, the batteries last for eight years. When batteries wear out, surgery is required to replace the unit or the batteries. Otherwise, the Backlofin is refilled via a syringe every six to eight months.

Sara decided to proceed. A test was scheduled.

Sara arrived at Baylor Hospital in Irving, TX, for the evaluation as a candidate for the pump. Faye Redding told us BCBS of Georgia had approved the device for Sara. The trial consisted of a spinal tap in which the medicine is sent to the spinal column.

I was at work when Joan called to report the evaluation results. "You won't believe this," she said. "Sara was able to lift her right leg and cross it during the test." Given the spasticity in the leg, this was amazing. The evaluation showed Sara to be an excellent candidate for the Backlofin pump.

Once again I thought about how Sara would not have had this device if we had simply opted to send her to a nursing home. I also wondered how many people already in nursing homes this instrument could help.

Sara's surgery was scheduled. It actually was a minor surgery with just an overnight stay. She was sore after the surgery, because the doctors had to cut through the muscles around the stomach to place the pump. She also had a small incision in the back into which the surgeon placed the catheter to deliver the medicine to the spinal column.

Sara recovered from the surgery very quickly and was back to normal in just a few days. We saw a noticeable change in Sara's ability with her right leg. Dr. Rappa wanted to incrementally increase Sara's dose to tune the device. Regulating the device was something that looked like a palm pilot. It would print out a three-page report telling virtually everything about the pump. In addition, the palm-like instrument programmed the pump and told it how much medicine to deliver.

Over time Dr. Rappa continued to adjust the device. It really improved Sara's life. It is hardly noticeable except to airport scanners. Incredibly with this device Sara does not need disability assistance to wheel her around the airport in a wheelchair. The only other drawback is the small chirping sound when the medicine in the pump gets low. When this happened the first time, I woke up and scanned the whole house looking for smoke detectors with low batteries. I found none. Later I went in search of low cell-phone batteries. The next day Sara informed me that she had scheduled an appointment because her pump was low on medicine and that it occasionally beeped. Little did she know that the night before I had lost four-hours sleep while she slept soundly!

Chapter 13

Ready for Discharge

Faye Redding called both Wayne Smith and me to tell us that BCBS of Georgia was ready to initiate the discharge of Sara from CNS. Wayne and I had already discussed that my insurance coverage had approximately 30 days of coverage for outpatient therapy. Wayne believed that Sara could benefit from another 30 days of coverage and approached Faye about using additional therapy two or three days a week. That would leverage the amount of time and help Sara transition. The outpatient coverage for medical necessity was ending, but the 30 days a year could be used to supplement this coverage, Faye and Wayne agreed. Faye told Wayne to just send the invoices to her at BCBS. All appeared to be great!

The daily trip from Mesquite to Irving was now down to just a couple of times a week. This really helped out from both expense and logistical standpoints, since the care involved two roundtrips to take Sara to and from outpatient therapy. The additional days would focus on educational and speech therapy.

Sara was doing extremely well in educational progress. She had spent three months as an in-patient at CNS and almost 12 months in out-patient therapy. The results were dramatic!

Sara was a little unsure about the approaching discharge, because it would be a big change. The situation was akin to graduating from school and realizing you have to get a job. While Sara was excited about the change, she told me that she would miss the people at CNS. I reassured her that we would go back and visit.

Discharge day finally arrived, so we had our discharge meeting. It lasted almost a two hours. Representatives from each of the five therapy areas presented their findings. Sara had progressed to a level of achievement I had originally thought unattainable. She maxed out on all of the tests from speech to education. While she had some issues with speech, the fact that she had not lost her cognitive abilities promised continued improvement. In education she had excelled in all areas. Interestingly in the beginning Sara didn't generally read an entire article in the paper. As she improved with her reading skills, she would read a headline and the funnies. Then she progressed to the point today where she reads articles and is now reading novels.

The physical therapist said Sara had progressed well. While she was still at risk of a fall, the therapists indicated she easily could ambulate. The therapists expressed concern that Sara needed continuing physical training to keep her in shape.

At the discharge meeting,Wayne had tears in his eyes. As a case manager he sincerely cared for his patients. His tears were for joy about Sara's progress as well as about sadness that she was leaving. Sara stood up and thanked Wayne and the team. She walked out of CNS just like Rachel, the therapist at Baylor, had predicted.

The best news is that Wayne hadn't seen everything yet! Sara still had a lot more to demonstrate to all of us.

Chapter 14

Other Insurance Issues

Faye Redding from BCBS of Georgia had told both Wayne Smith and me that Sara could use the 30 days of outpatient therapy for continuation of treatment at CNS. When Wayne sent her the invoices in late 2005, I received a numbing array of insurance papers denying the claim. We appeared to be in a game of submit and deny, submit and deny, until somebody blinked. Because of what Faye had said, I had full confidence that these invoices would be covered.

Meanwhile in my research on stroke treatment I found a new device for a hand splint. I contacted Wayne about the device. We had Sara tested for it. Joan took Sara to be tested on the device. The result showed Sara could be helped by it. We submitted a request to BCBS of Georgia to cover the $800 cost. A month went by; we heard nothing from the insurance carrier. I made 15 phone calls to both BCBS of Georgia and BCBS of Texas trying to find the progress on acquiring the device. Frustrated by the delay, I moved ahead to personally buy and pay for the device. Sara now was ready for the therapy sessions beginning in January 2006. Unfortunately, this is one of the few things that really didn't work out. Despite some initial successes, Sara's therapists determined it wouldn't help promote the use of her right arm and hand.

Since we had some days left for the outpatient therapy, Wayne and I consulted with Dr. Rappa. He wrote up authorizations for Sara to continue with physical, occupational, and speech therapy.

After several months Wayne contacted me about the outstanding bills for the 2005 and 2006 therapy sessions. I told him that I had received an EOB from BCBS of Georgia and that it was a typical denial. Wayne asked me to contact my insurance carrier to understand what was going on. I dug through a two-foot pile of invoices, medical slips, and other medical statements before I contacted BCBS of Georgia. I then sent emails to Faye with no response. I tried calling her and had no response. I then wrote an official appeal of the denials.

Surprise! The case worker I had dealt with in the beginning who had been so uncooperative was now back as my case worker. She told me these claims were denied. I told her to speak with Faye Redding and got no response. I finally sent a letter expressing my displeasure with having to deal with this individual. I received a call back from BCBS of Georgia. The person explained that I would be getting a new caseworker. I then asked about Faye Redding. I was told she was no longer employed by BCBS of Georgia.

So here I was with more than $19,000 in new medical bills that I was responsible for in additional to the other bills that I already had paid and had borrowed money to cover. I found the whole thing unbelievable. My appeal again was denied based on CNS not being part of the BCBS network.

At this point I hired an attorney to help me with a final appeal. I spent more than $5,000 to have the final appeal put together. It was a brilliantly crafted document that spelled out how I had been misled. After four letters back to understand the status of my final appeal, I received a call from BCBS of Georgia denying my final appeal. My lawyer told me any further legal fees on my part would be good money chasing bad money because the laws are stacked against the claimant in this type of medical appeal. When I appealed to my benefits team at Cingular, I was told that Cingular could not intervene because this was not allowed under the contract between Cingular and BCBS of Georgia.

In yet another case recently in 2007, Sara went to Baylor of Garland. Based on the problems she was having with her affected foot, which was curling in, the rehabilitation doctor authorized something called a Dynasplint. Baylor of Garland received authorization from my insurance company for the device; Sara started wearing it. Dynasplint is still trying to get paid for the device. I have made calls on their behalf.

All these problems leave me wondering how anyone would want to put up in dealing with the business interactions of these insurance companies.

Since the stroke Sara has never been able to place her right foot flat on the ground. The foot curls; thus she has trouble walking without assistance. Throughout the past two years this problem had gotten worse. After using the Dynasplint at night for about six weeks, Sara told me, "Look at what I can do." I turned to watch her walk with her foot flat on the floor. I was absolutely amazed! Here is a company that performed something just short of a miracle, yet they have to put up with insurance problems!

I'm bringing up all of the insurance problems in this section to help others understand they must be familiar with policies of their coverage and not to rely on someone acting as an agent of the insurance company. I hope that this story will help drive legislation to change the way that these insurance companies do business. I plan to lobby my congressional representative to force changes and to make the insurance companies accountable for their actions. Given the current political climate, I am certain that insurance companies will pay for their behavior.

Chapter 15

Driving and Working

Joan continued to support the household but was very optimistic about her and Welton being able to move back to their retirement home in Virginia. A year ago I would not have thought that this would be possible. I even had my doubts and spoke to Joan about the need to hire a nanny to help Sara with the kids and house. Joan was firm and told me that Sara would not need a nanny. I could see where Sara got her determination. Her mother was huge sources of this get-it-done approach.

Things started to change dramatically after one doctor's appointment. Dr. Rappa was doing a checkup on the Baclofin pump when he told Sara that she could start driving. Sara wasn't so sure, but Joan encouraged her. I even took Sara out to deserted areas to have her test drive. I told her she would need to drive with the left foot on a right-footed gas pedal. Sara actually started driving very well, but doing so was uncomfortable. I told her I would get a left-footed gas pedal for her car. This was an instant hit with her. She found driving to be very comfortable. Then with Joan at her side she started driving on side streets. This was the second time Joan and Welton got to teach their daughter to drive. The first time was when she was 16. Sara started driving the kids to school and her to the grocery store. The next thing I knew, she was gallivanting all over town to go shopping. I was very happy at the progress. Her ability to drive also meant Sara's parents could begin planning their return to their home.

The sense of freedom that Sara developed appeared to really boost her confidence. She actually drove better after the stroke than before it. However, she did not want to drive on the highway. Throughout the next several weeks, Sara started driving on highways in areas where no congestion existed. She would drive on a service road and then enter the highway and exit quickly. I asked her why she was doing this. She said she was "just practicing".

Tiffany received her learner's permit and could drive with a licensed driver over age 18 in the car. This was both a blessing and a problem. Now Sara had a new chauffeur, which took some of the pressure off of Sara. The problem was that it also took the pressure off of Sara to relearn to drive. She would rely on Tiffany to drive, which may have slowed her driving progress some.

The other problem involved the left-foot gas pedal. When Tiffany or I drove, we would take out the left-foot gas pedal. It had an easy release. However, it was difficult for Sara to put it back in. So she would drive with the left-foot pedal out. This didn't appear to be a problem. Welton even drove with the pedal in and out—however he found it. He even bumped into the garage wall with minor damage one time. Well, finally it happened. Sara got confused because the gas pedal kept changing between the right and left. She hit the gas pedal meaning to hit the break. My dad, his friend Richard, and I repaired the damage. It could have been worse. The car was still drivable! We adopted a new rule in the Culver household: If you take out the left-foot gas pedal, put it back in after your drive. Today, this is not as big of an issue, because Sara has developed the balance and dexterity to easily put the left-footed gas pedal back in place herself.

Within a couple of months, Sara was driving with no issues on the highway. As this freedom opened up the distances that she traveled, another problem emerged. A person with a disability and one arm can't hold up a map or directions in one hand and drive with the other hand. A couple of times, I was on the phone with Sara trying to help her with directions.

I was determined to get her a GPS in our next vehicle. Sara and I embarked on an expedition to look for a minivan to replace her older minivan. We finally settled on a Honda Odyssey because of the nicely integrated GPS and rear back-up camera. This was also a great experience because it showed how much Sara had progressed. She was a very active participant in the buying progress and a savvy consumer.

I initially was concerned about her driving, but I have been very impressed with her progress. Over time she has progressed and never overreached her abilities to safely drive. Truthfully she is a better driver than I am today. This new freedom has expanded her world dramatically.

She has returned to work at Eastfield College in the school's Learning Assistance Center. One day Sara took off and went to Eastfield on her own. She spoke with the LAC manager, filled out the application, and started working as a math tutor. This was a phenomenal achievement that could only occur through God's grace, strength, and support. As I mentioned previously, she never lost her higher math skills (calculus, trigonometry, etc.). With her improvements in communication skills and her newfound freedom to drive, she has built the confidence to go and help students. Since we still have two children at home, Sara only works a couple of days a week. This allows her to continue to support the kids and the house while she rebuilds her professional passion for teaching. After just four months on the job, she now has students requesting her. I have watched her work with the students as well as tutor our own kids in math. While she is only tutoring now, I am firmly convinced that she will teach in the classroom again some day.

Speaking of driving, Sara has really expanded her horizons. Tiffany played soccer for the Sting soccer club in Dallas. During a game, a college coach from Texas A&M Commerce while reviewing another player spotted Tiffany on the field. He told me "Tiffany's a junior, right?" I told him, "Well, not really. She is a senior. She wants to graduate a year early." The coach then asked if she wanted to play college soccer. I responded that we had talked about it but that she wanted to focus on academics so that could get in veterinarian school. He asked about her grades and I told him she had all A's in all honors classes and had a high SAT score when she took the exam entering seventh grade. The coach then asked, "What if she could do both?" I said maybe.

Sara had expressed concern about a 17-year old going off to college. The next day I received a call from the school's honors college. To make a long story short, Tiffany received an honors-college scholarship and is playing soccer for Texas A&M Commerce.

So what does this have to do with Sara? She didn't hesitate a moment to drive two hours to Commerce to help Tiffany get enrolled and to visit. This really got to me and helped me to understand how much the independence of a person with a disability boosts his or her confidence and quality of life.

In our community a local company advertises scooters for the elderly and disabled. In the past I dismissed these ads. After having experienced all this with Sara, I can see where the independence to get around one's home, a local store, and even the ability to drive has huge and profound impacts on the confidence of an individual.

Chapter 16

Where We Are Today

Despite the ups and downs since May 2004, I am very pleased to say that we lead a normal life. Our children have their mother back home, I have my wife back, and many students have Sara back in their lives to help them with their mathematics.

Sara is active in our church. I recently went on a mission trip to Guayaquil, Ecuador. Just two years ago I could not imagine being able to travel on such a trip and leave Sara at home in charge of the kids. Many times during these past five years I prayed just to have my wife be able to communicate with me. Joan and Welton have moved back to their retirement lake house in the mountains of Virginia; Joan returned to work part-time. They visit us several times a year to help out.

Sara is able to communicate very effectively. She also manages and organizes the household and our family. Sara is able to handle all the complexity that is associated with a fast-paced lifestyle. However, we will never return to the hurried pace we had before her stroke. Sara is exercising 30 minutes a day on the treadmill. She is even walking at a four-degree angle!

The bottom line is that God used Sara to touch my life and the lives of many others. He has demonstrated through her recovery His awesome power. He has answered the prayers of many through the almost five years since her stroke. I would tell anyone reading this story to consider what our family has been through and how faith in God, a faith-based relationship, and a church family helped Sara recover and our family become even stronger. I would encourage you to share this story with someone that has gone through a catastrophic event and use it as a testimonial to witness to them about what God can do in their lives, too. Just as important, help them understand that through prayer and faith in God, they can keep from giving up against insurmountable odds.

Sara's driver's license expired in March 2008. She drives all over the place and is comfortable in traffic on the highway or side streets. However, I was dreading the renewal process because of my concern that they may not be able to comprehend her abilities like I do. Sara wanted to go to the Texas Department of Public Safety office in Garland, TX, on her own. I refused and said I wanted to go along with her. I believed that I needed to be there to be her advocate. I had prayed that everything would go smoothly. When Sara finally got up to see the clerk, the conversation appeared to be a disaster. The clerk confirmed that Sara had suffered a stroke and was disabled. She indicated that Sara could not get her license renewed. I intervened and said that she had been driving for more than one-and-a-half years. The clerk also perceived that Sara had some speech problems. I explained that Sara could speak fine. She actually had improved a thousand percent but sometimes had to pause to recall a particular word. A supervisor (a woman who is probably an angel in disguise) intervened and took over the case. She asked all the questions the clerk did; Sara confirmed that she is able to communicate. The supervisor took Sara to the back to administer the written test. If Sara passed, she then would have to take the driving test. An eternity seemed to pass while Sara was taking the test. What would happen if she couldn't drive? Her independence would be gone! I believed this would be devastating to her. I sat down in the waiting room and prayed for God to intervene to help her. She had not studied or prepared for the written test. I told God that I didn't even know if I could pass it. Then my prayers were answered. Sara passed the written test. At that point I knew that she could pass the driving test, and she did. I felt like a huge weight had been lifted from me. On the way home, Sara told me, "I wasn't worried. I knew I would pass." She passed the road test with no problem. When she returned to the parking lot, I ran over to open her door. As she exited she said, "I failed". As my heart stopped, she grinned and said, "just kidding!" What sense of humor!

As time has gone by, Sara works more hours at Eastfield College's LAC tutoring math. She works three days a week. I believe the interaction with the students really helps her continue to improve her speech. I firmly believe she will be able to teach in the classroom in a couple of years. Sara has even been tutoring Tiffany for her college mathematics classes.

Joshua is now on his second tour of duty in Iraq. He returned home for two-weeks leave in February 2009 for the birth of his daughter, June. Since he is scheduled to be in Iraq through November 2009, Sara goes over to visit our daughter-in-law, Eva, the older granddaughter, Aja, and baby June. Realizing Sara is a grandmother amazes me. She is a great mother but is even better as a grandmother. The only problem is I get worn out on the picture thing—taking pictures, hanging them, etc. Well, I am very happy to do it for her.

Joan and Welton are doing great in their retirement home in the mountains of Virginia. My mother, Billie, went to be with the Lord in March 2008. This really affected Sara and made her very sad. I have been impressed with my wife. She goes out on a regular basis and puts new flowers on my mother's gravesite.

I could end this chapter by saying that we are back to being a normal family. However, given what we have been through and the blessings that God has bestowed on us, I would say that we are not a *normal* family. We are an example of what faith can do in the lives of a family.

Inevitably we all will face death one day. Probably some day some type of catastrophe will significantly alter your family's lifestyle or one member individually. When faced with these dire consequences, look up and ask God for guidance and support. What can seem devastating can turn into a blessing by faith and acceptance of Jesus Christ as your Lord and Savior.

I wrote this book to inspire others. I also wrote this book to say hope exists and is very real. We have hope in this lifetime and hope for an everlasting life free of pain and suffering— and full of pleasure and joy in being with our Lord.

Family Photo Album

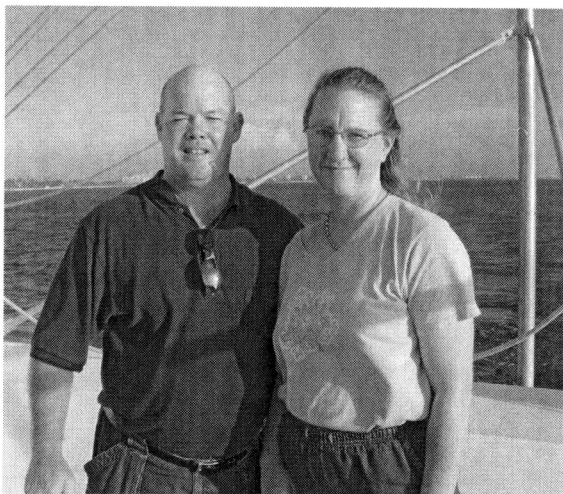

Tim and Sara Culver visit Aruba
during their first vacation after her stroke.

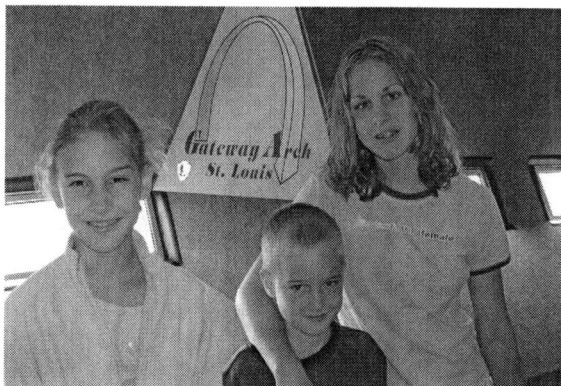

Three of Tim and Sara's children:
Tiffany, Jeremy, and Tricia

Tim, Welton, Joan and Sara enjoy an outing together.

Sara and son Joshua celebrate
his military service in Iraq.

Sara in 1986 before stroke

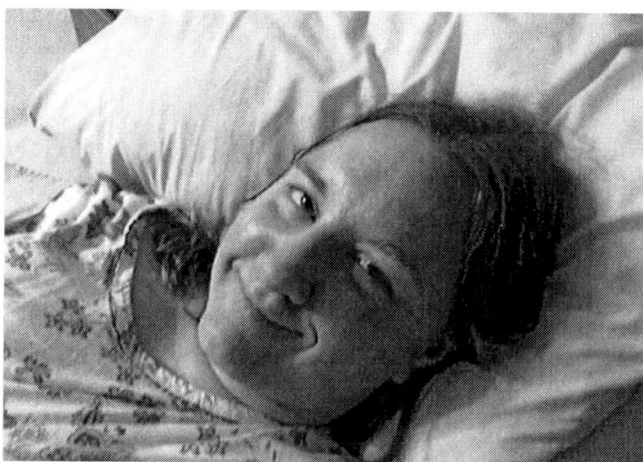
Sara at Baylor Rehabilitation following stroke

Breinigsville, PA USA
24 January 2010
231279BV00008B/85/P